PERGAMON INTERNATIONAL LIBRARY
of Science, Technology, Engineering and Social Studies

The 1000-volume original paperback library in aid of education,
industrial training and the enjoyment of leisure.

Publisher: Robert Maxwell, M.C.

SPAIN:
A BRIEF HISTORY

D1351384

THE PERGAMON TEXTBOOK
INSPECTION COPY SERVICE

An inspection copy of any book published in the Pergamon International Library will gladly
be sent to academic staff without obligation for their consideration for course adoption or
recommendation. Copies may be retained for a period of 60 days from receipt and returned
if not suitable. When a particular title is adopted ~~~~~~~~~~~~ for class use
an~~~~~~ on copy may
be~~~~~~ ggestions for
re~~~~~~ Library.

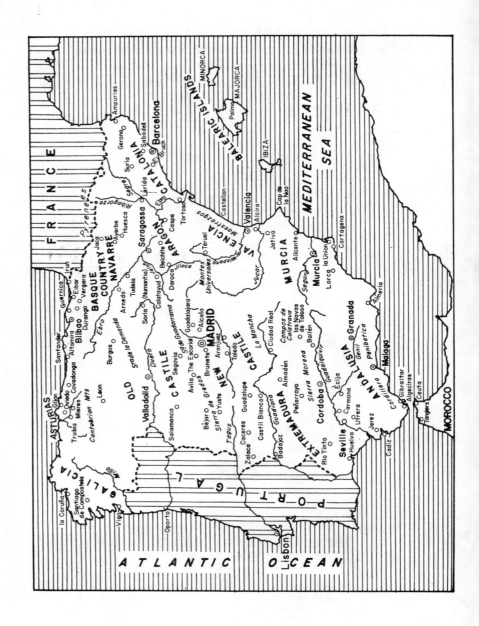

SPAIN:
A BRIEF HISTORY

SECOND EDITION

by PIERRE VILAR
DIRECTOR OF STUDIES AT THE ECOLE
PRATIQUE DES HAUTES ETUDES, PARIS

Translated by BRIAN TATE

PERGAMON PRESS

OXFORD · NEW YORK · TORONTO · SYDNEY
PARIS · FRANKFURT

U.K.	Pergamon Press Ltd., Headington Hill Hall, Oxford OX3 0BW, England
U.S.A.	Pergamon Press Inc., Maxwell House, Fairview Park, Elmsford, New York 10523, U.S.A.
CANADA	Pergamon of Canada Ltd., 75 The East Mall, Toronto, Ontario, Canada
AUSTRALIA	Pergamon Press (Aust.) Pty. Ltd., 19a Boundary Street, Rushcutters Bay, N.S.W. 2011, Australia
FRANCE	Pergamon Press SARL, 24 rue des Ecoles, 75240 Paris, Cedex 05, France
WEST GERMANY	Pergamon Press GmbH, 6242 Kronberg-Taunus, Pferdstrasse 1, West Germany

Copyright © 1967   Pergamon Press Ltd.

First edition 1967
Second edition 1977

Library of Congress Cataloging in Publication Data

Vilar, Pierre, 1906–
Spain, a brief history.

(Pergamon Oxford Spanish series)
Translation of Histoire de l'Espagne.
Includes index.
1. Spain—History. I. Title.
DP68.V5513   1977   946   77–4392
ISBN 0 08 021462 2 (Hardcover)
ISBN 0 08 021461 4 (Flexicover)

(This work is based on the sixth French edition of *Histoire de l'Espagne* in the "Que sais-je" paperback edition of the Presses Universitaires de France (1965) and the Spanish Edition (1960). The metric measurements have not been converted. Metric ton = 0·984 British ton, 1·102 U.S.A. ton; the hectare = 2·471 acres. Although these measurements were introduced into Spain in 1859, several old weights and measures are still widely used. They are: the *quintal* = 220·4 lb avoirdupois; the *libra* = 1·014 lb avoirdupois; the *arroba* for wine = 3·5 imperial gal; the *arroba* for oil = 2·75 imperial gal; the *fanega* = 1·5 imperial bushels; the *fanega de tierra* = 1·59 acres; *Translator's note*.)

Printed in Great Britain by Biddles Ltd., Guildford, Surrey

CONTENTS

TRANSLATOR'S NOTE

The revision of the section dealing with the régime of General Franco was effected by Professor Vilar before the Caudillo's death on 20 November 1975 at the age of 82. Since then Don Juan Carlos has been installed as monarch and the government has been reshuffled to bring a relatively unknown Falangist bureaucrat, Adolfo Suarez, to the premiership. Many ex-ministers have withdrawn to form their own political parties. All the major parties in opposition, including the communists, have now presented themselves successfully for official legalisation and await the outcome of the first free elections for forty years to a newly styled two-chamber assembly. The King and the prime minister have walked delicately along the path to Western style democracy, but the journey is by no means complete. Hesitant liberalisation (punctuated by sharp repressive measures) has provoked a guarded optimism. One thing seems certain, the referendum held at the end of 1976 showed that the voter wants to turn his back on the immediate past. But what part will his country play now in Western Europe?

CHAPTER 1

THE PHYSICAL BACKGROUND
AND EARLY CIVILISATION

I. THE PHYSICAL BACKGROUND

The Atlantic, the Mediterranean, the Pyrenean chain: within such clearly marked boundaries, the physical background seems to offer to its inhabitants a distinctive setting for a unique destiny and a particular historical identity. Indeed, the off-centre position of the Peninsula, its isolation by the Pyrenees, the significant peculiarities of structure and climate, the lure of certain valuable resources, have always contrived to present to Europe an Iberia in possession of a striking and subtle originality. It is not, whatever one may have said, "African". Certain natural constants have moulded this massive peninsula—this minor continent—into a distinct historical unit.

Let us not conclude that the Iberian world is a closed one, nor that it has offered to those human beings who landed there conditions particularly favourable to the creation of a community of interests. On the one hand, it offers a welcoming coastline to all sorts of external influences; but, on the other, to those ready to penetrate more deeply, it quickly sets up multiple barriers of sierra and plateau, rude of climate and shallow in resources. In complete contrast to France, Iberia, less well defended, but extremely well articulated about its river network, does not possess any coherent natural system of communication. There is no geographical centre to play the role of London or Paris. Narrow gorges bar practically all the major valleys at the edge of the plateaux. It is tempting to repeat the well-worn phrase that Spain is "invertebrate", but it would be truer to say that she has suffered, during the development

of her human resources, from the excessive space taken up by the
bony skeleton of her relief within the physical structure, at the
expense of the organs of production, assimilation, exchange and
human activity in general. Between the unbroken barrier of the
central Pyrenees and the equally challenging crests which dominate
Granada and Almería, stretches a mountainous and continental
Iberia, difficult of entry, and therefore *isolated*, hard of climate, and
therefore *poverty-stricken in her ways of life.*

Isolation and poverty—contemporary literature has often taken
these two conditions as underlying the spiritual values of the
Spanish people. From these may be derived "the essence of Spain"
according to Unamuno, its "profundities" according to Réné
Schwob, and its "virginity" according to Ganivet or Frank. It is
undeniable that the man of the meseta will play a great role, indeed
the leading role, in the story we intend to outline. And it is from
the nature of his country that he has drawn his passion for independence, his warlike courage and his asceticism, his taste for political
domination and his disdain for commercial gain, his aspiration to
forge and maintain the vital unity of the Peninsula. But is not this
aspiration merely the emotional reflection, simple yet confused, of
a human need? Isolated, central Spain would lead a precarious
existence: it lacks resources and supports few people. Communications with the outside world are poor; material and spiritual
advances are only slowly absorbed. To keep contact, to maintain
her vitality, to play any sort of part in the outside world, central
Spain must associate herself closely with the magnificent Peninsular
coastline, so alive, so ready to assimilate and so significantly placed
in relation to the Old and New Worlds. From the high meseta of
Soria, Antonio Machado contrasted (in order, of course, to complete) the "arid, warlike" Spain with the other rich, luxuriant
Spain, "mother of all fruits", orchard of the Golden Apples of
antiquity, garden of the caliphs, adored by popular tradition and
romantic literature. And how can one forget the glorious girdle of
Iberian ports from which there set out for the conquest of the East
and then the West the merchants and sailors of Catalonia, Andalusia,
Majorca, Portugal, Valencia and the Basque provinces?

Alas, this happy, vital Iberia (in a manner classic to the Mediterranean periphery) resents the power exerted by the hinterland. Physically, because of the relief, the shape and alignment of the valleys, the coastal fringe, isolated or broken up, turns its back on the central mesetas. Theodor Fischer showed this for Portugal a long time ago. It is also true (indeed truer, since the central meseta is irregular in its relief) of the small coastal units of the Spanish Levant. This is why so many maritime regions of Spain have had an independent history. On the other hand, none of these petty powers, whose successes were usually in the economic sphere, ever had enough territorial base or political energy to pull along with it the whole Peninsula. The history of Iberia has been a ceaseless struggle between the will to unite, located generally in the centre, and the no less vital tendency—rooted in geography—to dispersion.

Thus the present, like the past, stems from this contradictory nature. The vastness, the aridity, the impossible relief of the Spanish meseta, taken together with a certain technical and social backwardness, impose upon the nation up to 1960 an average wheat yield of less than ten quintals per hectare. Can this satisfy for long a population which has risen from 17 to 35 million in a matter of a hundred years? Inversely, where have the so expensive, but so specialised, products of the *huerta* lands drained away to? Which will come out on top in the end, the spiritual and economic archaism of the far-flung country areas, or the seething innovations of port and metropolis? Let us not forget that Catalans and Basques, that is, the Spaniards most accessible to foreign contact, have for nearly a century felt an inclination to desert the national community. Clearly this is a crisis that must be resolved, and a synthesis re-established. And if certain individuals (this happens above all in Castile) have preached as a solution to the grave problems facing the people the solitary pride of isolation and the single-minded cult of individuality, modern life will reply to them: Gibraltar, Tangiers, the Canary Islands and the Balearics, submarine bases, aerodromes, Río Tinto copper and Suria potash. Economically and strategically Spain cannot remain indifferent to the harsh realities of the present day. Between Africa and Europe, the Atlantic and the Mediterranean, the Peninsula is a meeting point, a cross-roads—a strangely cluttered cross-roads, practically a road-block—but nevertheless a place of contact into which from remote times men and civilisation have infiltrated, a place where they have clashed and left their mark.

II. PRIMITIVE MAN AND EARLY CIVILISATION

These are the reasons why there is no more a Spanish race than a French race, in the anthropological sense.

The settlement of Spain dates from an early age. Palaeolithic remains in abundance are spread over sites which have a great future, like that at Madrid. At Altamira, the Cantabrians have left "the Sistine Chapel of prehistoric art" (Magdalanian). At the meeting-point of the Neolithic and Copper Ages, Andalusia became once more the site of extensive human development. It is almost impossible to guess what lies behind the first known names given in the texts. The very word "Iberian" is not completely clear. It is applied to an African people of a Berber type who infiltrated up to the Pyrenees along the Levant coast and whose customs can be fairly exactly described. Scholars have given up the attempt to identify the Iberians with the Basques, whose past may go back as far as the great Oriental migrations. Within Spanish ethnography, the Celtic element is by no means negligible—the fusion of the Iberians and Celts (Celtiberians) on the meseta is characterised by distinct traits, and the Celt properly speaking is the dominant type in the far corners of Galicia.

From the beginning of the historical era there follows an unbroken succession of visitors to the Spanish Levant from the other end of the Mediterranean. Rome after the Punic Wars never completely abandoned the idea of controlling the whole Peninsula—but she took a long time to impose her authority on the meseta. She found there unique forms of resistance which became very familiar later on, the guerrillas of Viriatus and the implacable defensive zeal of the besieged towns. For twenty years, on the highest point of the meseta, Numantia was the nightmare of the Roman soldier; and in 133 B.C. it preferred to commit collective suicide rather than surrender. Gradually, however, the coastal regions, quickly Romanised, exerted pressure on the rest of the country to bring about one of the most successful periods of Peninsula history, at least in appearance.

This Golden Age occurred in the first two centuries A.D. The Spanish mines were exploited unceasingly. Roads and bridges, clumsy or imposing, ran out to Galicia and Cantabria. The great hydraulic structures often improperly attributed to the Arabs date from Roman times. Andalusia became Rome's granary, and Spain with its riches sent its most brilliant sons to the metropolis— Quintilian, Martial, Lucan, Seneca, the great emperors Hadrian and Trajan. It is still an open question whether the Roman superstructure really transformed the old tribal life or whether the economic yield of slavery did not decline earlier than was thought. Nevertheless, it is evident that even if the Roman system revealed signs of decadence from the third century onwards, and although the barbarians arrived in the fifth century, it still retained through these violent times its essential qualities, and did not collapse completely until A.D. 711 under the impact of Islam.

Christianity and the Church had been in great part the guarantors of its survival. The first invading waves of Alani, Suevi and Vandals destroyed a great deal, but swiftly passed through. The Visigoths from Gaul arrived, already largely Romanised. It was their religion —Arrianism—that really prolonged internal strife. When their King Reccared became converted to Catholicism, a great new epoch seemed about to open (A.D. 589). The Visigothic kings chose Toledo as their capital and brought an Iberian unity independent of any foreign empire. Latins and Goths progressively discarded their initial differences and a celebrated common code—the *Liber Judiciorum*—was drawn up by the clergy, while Isidore of Seville in his encyclopaedic work strove to preserve the spiritual heritage of antiquity. In fact it was the last glow of a civilisation, not the début of a new era; and it was not long before society was split by political and social differences. Slaves and settlers suffered miserably; religious and racial quarrels fermented once again; the Jews were persecuted, the nobles intrigued. Finally, as allies of one of the many parties, the Moslem Africans crossed the straits and brusquely changed the course of Spanish history.

Before moving on to that most remarkable period of history which begins with the Islamic invasion, it has been necessary to measure beforehand what had sedimented out of civilisations prior to the Medieval Period. With a long and brilliant prehistory, an exceptionally fertile and lasting period of Romanisation, an active part in the formation of Christendom, the Peninsula yields to none amongst the Mediterranean nations, all so well favoured, in respect of antiquity and an unbroken thread of civilised life.

CHAPTER 2

THE MAIN LINES OF THE PAST: THE MIDDLE AGES

I. MOSLEM SPAIN

1. ISLAM, ADVANCE AND RETREAT

Invaded in A.D. 711 by the Berber Tariq, the Peninsula was conquered in seven years—not without difficulty, let it be understood. Ultimately authority took root in Cordoba. Abd-al-Rahman I (756–88) an exiled Omayyad, broke the link of Spain with the East; Abd-al-Rahman III (912–61) proclaimed himself caliph, and Cordoba became the capital of the West. In spite of this, from the end of the tenth century onwards, the Christians reoccupied part of the north of Spain. Towards the year 1000 Al-Mansur "the Victorious" was still launching against them his destructive *razzias*. But thirty years later the caliphate crumbled away and twenty-three *taifas*—kingdoms or republican oligarchies—replaced it. The Christians meanwhile moved inexorably further south. On two occasions, nevertheless, Islam counter-attacked, thanks to the Berber sects from Africa: first the Almoravids (Sagrajas, 1086), then the Almohads (1172). In 1212, at Las Navas de Tolosa, the latter were checked. From that point on the Reconquest accelerated, leaving in existence through the fourteenth and fifteenth centuries the kingdom of Granada athwart the Sierra Nevada, and, moreover, many forms of Moorish life in the reconquered territories.

Spanish Islam exercised therefore an influence lasting from three to eight centuries according to region. In weighing up this influence, our minds have long been accustomed to making simple value judgements: either northern Barbarians against Andalusian sophistication,

7

or southern Barbarians who left a new-born civilisation in ruins. In this form the debate is of little interest, and by now has been left behind. Scholarly investigation has striven to isolate the positive facts and lasting influences.

2. THE BALANCE SHEET OF ISLAMIC INFLUENCE

On several counts the invasion was undoubtedly destructive; but no-one can deny the splendour given to Andalusia by her eastern lords. They did not "create", as has been said for a long time, an irrigation system and a prosperous agriculture, but they completed, improved and embellished the work of the Romans, introducing from Africa and Persia new fruits and as yet unknown horticultural practices. And, likewise, if urban life had shone in Roman times it triumphed in Moorish Spain. The present Moroccan *medinas* (refuges, moreover, for many Andalusians) allow us to imagine what Cordoba, Seville, Toledo, Almería and Granada were like from the tenth to the fourteenth centuries: artisans working in leather, metal, furniture, china, wool and silk; traders organised under a precise and complex municipal control; above all this, the magnificence of palaces, mosques, schools and libraries. Nor did this occur only in the brief period of the caliphate—the geographer Idrisi, the philosopher Averroes lived not in the tenth, but in the twelfth century, at the close of which the Giralda was built in Seville. And the Alhambra, so often selected as a symbol of Hispano-Arabic civilisation, is in effect its last reflection, dating mainly from the fourteenth and fifteenth centuries.

How could such a period so brilliant and prolonged disappear without a trace? Amongst the Andalusian peoples one can point to Arabic traits still alive in popular art (carpets, ceramics), in music, family customs, temperament and religion. But there is a case for proceeding with a certain prudence. The term "Arab" evokes a misleading idea of racial influence which was surely limited. Berber immigration—much less alien to the ancient Spanish stock—was certainly considerable, and multiple contacts quickly created a relatively coherent Hispano-Moorish group. Moorish Spain was in fact a crucible in which were fused the contributions of diverse cultures—the mosque at Cordoba, the Alhambra at Granada, harmonious yet composite creations, prove the case at the two extremes of her development. The products of this crucible filter across into Christian Europe—scholastic philosophy, romanesque art, the school of medicine at Montpellier, the lyric poetry of the troubadours and the mystical poetry of Dante.

How did this happen? The fact is that the two worlds were by no means separate. Between small Christian and Moorish units wars broke out, but there were also exchanges, intrigues, treaties and mutual compliments. The rights of the vanquished were fairly rapidly guaranteed, and each society possessed a hierarchy. Amongst the Moslems, Arab chieftains, soldiers, then Berbers, Christian renegades and local Christians of unchanged faith called Mozarabs; amongst the Christians, nobles and clergy, "Old Christian" commoners, resettled Mozarabs, converts or "New Christians", *mudéjares* who had kept their Islamic faith, customs and judges. To this add the Jews, long revered, and let us not forget the slaves. In cultural matters, the exchange was continuous. There were Christians who knew Arabic (*algarabiados*), and Moslems who knew romance (*ladinos*), while one of the kings of the Reconquest was to found a triple university, Arabic, Hebrew and Christian.

In short, there existed in the Middle Ages an active and innovating Spanish version of Islam whose thought, complexity and luxuriance contributed, no less than the Christian Reconquest, to the successes of future Spain.

II. THE RECONQUEST

1. THE ADVANCE OF THE RECONQUEST

After the symbolic victory of Covadonga (722) there arose in the first half of the eighth century a compact mountainous Christian state in Asturias, Cantabria and Galicia. The Moors hardly settled north of the line Coimbra, Toledo, Guadalajara, and the depopulated plateaux of Leon and Burgos were abandoned to seasonal *razzias*. But from the middle of the eighth to the middle of the ninth century, internal divisions put the Asturian kings on the defensive.

This defensive attitude between 785 and 811 nevertheless favoured the Reconquest, allowing Frankish advances on the eastern side. These were mainly successful in present-day northern Catalonia, where a Frankish "march" was founded with the counts of Barcelona in command. In the Pyrenees, witness Roncesvaux, nuclei of Basques and Navarrese struggled independently.

After 840 the Asturian kingdom moved over again to the offensive, reaching the Douro and locating its capital in Leon. Shortly afterwards, however, a dissident count (932–70) founded Castile in the Burgos area whilst a Navarrese kingdom in the Pyrenees reached the upper Ebro at Tudela. This progress was halted by Al-Mansur around the year 1000.

The fall of the Cordoban caliphate allowed Castile to further its earlier triumphs—the Christians crossed the central Sierra and took Toledo (1085). Then came the arrival of the Almoravids, resisted only by the Cid who carved out a domain for himself around Valencia (1095). This was, however, lost at his death, and feuds sprang up again in Castile.

The twelfth century belongs to Aragon and her victories. This small Pyrenean kingdom centred on Saragossa in 1118 under Alfonso the Battler. He seized the Moorish strongholds south of the Ebro, Calatayud and Daroca, and then linked himself by marriage to the county of Barcelona, which in its turn had reached Tortosa at the Ebro estuary. Teruel was founded by the Aragonese in 1170, but they then turned their interest northwards for a time to the French Midi.

The Almohad threat in the early thirteenth century provoked a vigorous reaction on the part of the Christians, leading to a general co-operation in 1212. For the future Reconquest, Las Navas de Tolosa, a victory resulting from this co-operation, was a military event of the highest consequence. From then on the western kingdom of Portugal moved to the conquest of its southern provinces; in Castile, Saint Ferdinand arrived at Cordoba in 1236, Seville in 1248; in Aragon James I, the Conqueror, took the Balearics between

1229 and 1235, Valencia in 1238, then Játiva and Alcira, and later Murcia. Around 1270 there only remained in Moslem hands the kingdom of Granada and a few shreds of territory in the area of Huelva.

From 1270 to the end of the fifteenth century the Reconquest slowed down. Portugal turned to the Atlantic, Aragon to the Mediterranean; Castile was torn by dynastic struggles, although she never ceased to brush with the Moors of Granada and Africa. By the end of the Middle Ages, the heroic period of the Reconquest had passed. This period possessed other characteristics which led to consequences to be dealt with later.

2. THE HERITAGE OF THE RECONQUEST

The slow speed of the Reconquest is an important feature in itself. A rapid expulsion of the Infidel would have changed the fate of Spain; it would not have moulded her structure, her spirit and her customs as did a crusade of several centuries. Clearly the leaders of a fragmented Spain were not continuously guided by a lucid awareness of their aims across a period sown with disconnected events. The pressure of necessity in a poor country with a rising population made the Reconquest everywhere into a continuous process of colonisation as well as a Holy War. Medieval Spanish society was based on the demands of the Faith and the need to expand.

Between 711 and 1492 Spain—and above all Castile—was to be a society constantly in arms. The fighting class naturally acquired for itself the major role; thus the power of the barons was greater here than anywhere else and the lower nobility more numerous. The former did not have its roots in the great fiefs as in France—the tiny kingdoms of the Reconquest had no room for divisions of this type. But they had their great nobles, the king's right-hand men in battle, whose individual valour and substantial following strengthened their spirit of independence and led to the pursuit of often audacious personal policies in war or intrigue with the enemy. In this way Count Fernán González founded Castile; and the Cid, an even more impressive example, became an arbiter of Moorish disputes and

governed Valencia almost like a king. Later, during the great
advances to the south in the thirteenth century, and particularly
following the Castilian conquest of Andalusia, the rise of the great
nobility was of a different kind. The kings themselves contributed
to its formation through the distribution of immense domains, entire villages and vast amounts of property. These great families still
remain on many counts masters of rural estates in certain provinces,
significant figures in the Court, and linked to power through
tradition.

The role of the lower nobility, although very different, was no
less impressive. From the beginning of the Reconquest, small armies
of *infanzones* and *caballeros* followed the king or the great lords.
Rich enough to fit themselves out for war, these owners of small
estates (*hidalgos* or "sons of something", as they were later to be
called) remained overall less than wealthy, and were later joined by
the younger sons of great families whom the system of *mayorazgo*
or primogeniture, eventually of general application, turned towards the Church or a military career. They were to staff the armies
of Flanders or Italy; and the "Conquest" of the Indies, a natural
consequence of the "Reconquest" of the Middle Ages, was achieved
by a social class whose only *raison d'être* was war. They would later
print across the face of Spain (whose decadence denied them employment abroad) their fantasies and nostalgic search for adventure,
their pride and refusal to renounce their position. They would become Don Quixote or the *pícaro*, and later the anachronistic squires,
admirable or ridiculous, of nineteenth-century novelists. Even today, beneath the *petit bourgeois* guise is it not possible to detect in
the country landowner, the small-town lawyer, the student or
soldier exploited by the Francoist *movimiento*, the same attitude of
the *hidalgo* towards class, the same hopes and aspirations, the same
reaction to work and the practical life, the same ideals, which are
nothing more than a refusal to abdicate?

These observations apply equally to the clergy, accustomed by
centuries of Reconquest to provide the ideological framework for
an entire society. Like the nobility they were divided into a rich and
powerful aristocracy and an indigent multitude, both suffused with

a sense of importance and authority. A vigorous tradition had forged the Spanish clergy into a militant, even military force, undeterred (indeed often the contrary) by the idea of armed struggle for the faith and its supporters, and arrogating to itself the spiritual and in part the lay direction of society.

It must be affirmed straight away that the dominant role of the clergy and nobility in no way meant the social or political demise of other levels of society. There can be no doubt that the Reconquest itself was responsible for a fortunate equilibrium. The demands of military action and resettlement imprinted on the society of the Reconquest its particular traits. On the one hand war maintained the throne in high enough prestige to restrain the emergence of feudalism, on the other popular elements were able to acquire exceptional privileges. The work on the land, the defence of reconquered strongpoints occasioned many personal or collective concessions of the type of the *behetría* (protection of an individual or a group by a noble of his choice) or of the *cartapuebla* (charters for resettlement). On this basis, even after the development of the feudal system the rural and urban communities became powerful and relatively independent. Later, with the expansion of the Reconquest, various reconquered groups (mozarabs, jews, *mudéjares*) received in their turn statutes and *fueros*. In the end medieval Spanish society was ruled by a complex series of *fueros* which have left their mark. To this must be added a new phenomenon from the end of twelfth century. When the congenital economic weaknesses of Castile slowed the expansion of the middle classes to a stop, there arose on the periphery of the Peninsula—Portugal, Catalonia, Valencia, the Balearics—veritable bourgeois nuclei, trading republics *à l'italienne*. It is worth while having a closer look at the above medieval phenomena to which the non-noble classes had the opportunity of making a contribution and whose traces have not yet disappeared.

One may cite the communal economic habits of the countryside: common rights in woodland and pasture, periodic sharing of fields and harvests, pastoral "collectives" in high valleys, transhumance groups, communal management of water supplies with remarkably sound regulations. Spanish agrarian "collectivism" remained in opposition to private encroachment well into the nineteenth century, and even in the twentieth the debate has not finished.

Then there are the municipal traditions of the villages, towns and cities, resting either on the elementary *concejo* or sovereign assembly of the inhabitants, or later on more limited gatherings, not forgetting the trend of such municipalities to federation; witness the *hermandades* of Castile, the Cantabrian and Basque port groupings, the ring of Catalan towns around Barcelona which through some legal fiction were given the name of "streets" of the capital city. This local vitality, this "cantonalism" with its dream of federation, remains a constant in Spanish politics. Lastly there are the famous "Cortes" which represent, together with the throne and its natural advisers (nobles and clergy) the popular element in the nation. This typical institution of medieval Spain is a remarkably precocious example in the history of representative assemblies. It emerged more than likely in Leon, before the end of the twelfth century, but functioned normally from mid-thirteenth century in all Spanish kingdoms—Castile, Aragon, Valencia, Catalonia, Navarre. More frequently summoned and consequently less revolutionary than the French States General, the Cortes recorded the royal succession, received the royal oath to respect the *fueros*, voted subsidies, and (according to the region, before or after this act, a not unimportant variation) put forward complaints (*agravios, greuges*). This has provoked talk of medieval Spanish "democracy". As long as this is understood in a precisely limited sense, it is true that few peoples have so generously shared in the government of their country than the Spaniards in the Middle Ages, and it is right that this should be remembered, for it has played a not insignificant part in the psychology of Spanish politics.

It is above all in the thirteenth century that Spain knew its happiest moments. In Castile Saint Ferdinand reigned from 1230 to 52. No less Christian than his cousin Saint Louis, but more practical, he limited the idea of crusade to the borders of Spain, and with an open mind he called himself "King of the three Faiths". In Aragon ruled the energetic Catalan, "En Jaume", James the Conqueror, fighter,

poet, brutal, courtly and unscrupulous, but at the same time surrounded by saints like Ramon de Penyafort, Peter Nolasco, and the
extraordinary Ramon Llull. Islam fell back, the cathedrals soared up,
Christianity triumphed.

There is one reservation. Spain of the Reconquest disintegrated
rather than cohered. Leon, from the ninth to the eleventh, and
Castile to the middle of the twelfth century, never failed to lay
claim to the Visigothic heritage; their kings maintained the title
"Emperors of all Spain". But the idea shattered against reality.
Geographically, the struggle was originally led from out of mountainous areas, physically isolated; historically, the war against the
Moors favoured attempts at independent rule. Castile broke away
from Leon, the Cid nearly created a domain in Valencia, Portugal
developed independently. To the east the thirteenth-century Reconquest acquired a federal shape—Valencia and Majorca were
raised to the status of kingdoms beside Aragon and the County of
Catalonia: the very division of Moorish Spain into *taifas* encouraged
this fragmentation. Asturias, Leon and Castile, Galicia and Portugal,
Navarre, Sobrarbe, Aragon, Ribagorza, the Catalan counties
coalesced or dispersed according to the rhythm of marriage and
family succession. Each accumulated and preserved the fame of its
titles and its battle honours, a mistrust of its neighbours, an indi-
vidualism exacerbated by free municipalities and noble adventurers.

Above all this, it is true, shone the unity of the faith and the
spirit of the crusade, the feeling of a Christian community set
against the Moors which local accident or circumstantial alliance
could not overshadow. But one can recognise here a sign (perhaps
one of the most deeply rooted sources) of a new duality in the
Spanish situation—on the one hand an inclination to the particular,
to infranational ties; on the other a propensity to supranational
ideals and passions. It is hard to locate the Spanish conscience between these two extremes, and the indecision is still present. In the
thirteenth century the main fissures persisted, despite some necessary
simplifications of the pattern, like the union of Aragon and Catalonia
in 1137 and that of Leon and Castile in 1230. Even leaving aside
Navarre (tied for a time by a dynastic accident to France) and the as

yet unconquered kingdom· of Granada, one cannot fail to notice a serious tripartite division in Iberia between Portugal, Castile, and the Aragonese–Catalan–Valencian "federation" in the east, a division all the more threatening inasmuch as it corresponds to three human temperaments and three natural geographical areas: the Atlantic, the meseta and the Mediterranean. The insertion of the Spanish Lower Middle Ages into this Peninsular tryptych is to have a considerable influence on the future of the country.

III. THE END OF THE MIDDLE AGES: CENTRIFUGAL AND CENTRIPETAL TENDENCIES

1. Centrifugal tendencies in the fourteenth century

The fourteenth century appeared to threaten the future of the Reconquest and Peninsular unification—only Castile pursued the fight against the Moors. But its political efficiency was undermined by dynastic crisis and nobiliary revolts—the struggle between the heirs of Alfonso X (1275–95), the minorities of Ferdinand IV and Alfonso XI (1312–25), the tragic duel between Peter the Cruel and his bastard brother, Henry of Trastamara (1350–69), and the claims of the House of Lancaster to the Castilian throne.

During this time Portugal spread its wings independently of the fate of the Peninsula as a whole. In 1383 a revolution swept the House of Avis to the throne; in 1385 the battle of Aljubarrota brushed aside Castilian intervention in this matter. From then on the royal dynasty and the trading bourgeoisie were to prepare the great series of navigations.

The "Crown of Aragon" (ill-named since it included, besides the impoverished landlocked kingdom, the rich maritime regions, and also because its sovereigns were Catalans) experienced a parallel attraction to the Mediterranean. The power of the ports, the commerce of the Levant (highly developed in the thirteenth century), the good fortune of the dynasty—from 1276 to 1410 seven kings of not inconsiderable prowess succeeded one another without difficulty—all this raised Aragon quickly to the level of a great Mediterranean power. Her kings attacked Tunis in 1280, intervened in Sicily, acquired rights over Sardinia and Corsica, fought at the side of Venice against Pisa and Genoa, established factories in the Levant and inherited the Morea and the Duchy of Athens from the Catalan adventurers who had torn them from Byzantium. Barcelona with its cathedral and the church of Our Lady of the Sea (Santa María del Mar), with its town hall of the Council of a Hundred (Consell de Cent), the Exchange of its maritime consulate, the palace which served as the seat of the permanent directorate of its "Corts" (the "Generalitat") not far from the residence of the kings of Aragon, all this preserves in the heart of an exciting old city the memory of a glorious past which has also fed the pride of more recent regionalist movements. In this expansion of Aragon may be found the origins of later Spanish interests in Naples and Italy. Clearly the fourteenth century must not be forgotten if one is to understand certain significant future events: the independence of Portugal, the multiple concerns of the Spanish Empire, and the resistance of the Catalans to Castilian hegemony.

2. CENTRIPETAL TENDENCIES IN THE FIFTEENTH CENTURY

(a) The decadence of Catalonia

The prosperity of the Levant was, in fact, brief. Before the end of the fourteenth century Majorca had lost a third of its ships and almost all its merchant companies. Thanks to the hinterland of the *huerta*, Valencia continued to be rich. But the homeland of the *casa comtal*, Catalonia, very soon revealed signs of exhaustion. The most obvious were demographic: hunger, plague, earthquakes, etc., between 1333 and 1521 prevented Catalonia reaching the high point of the thirteenth century (when it was more than likely overpopulated).

Out of this sprang a widespread agrarian conflict. The peasants wanted a higher wage because of the labour shortage; they wanted to work the abandoned farmhouses (*masies*). The landlords brandished their ancient privileges, the right of *prendre e mal tractar*, of *remença*, collectively known as the "evil customs" ("*mals usos*"). From 1380 to 1480 the agrarian revolt gradually changed from a spontaneous and mystical uprising into organised political groupings, then to armed struggle, thus undermining the bases of the Catalan social structure.

From 1350, urban growth withered, belying official forecasts, and after 1380 there followed financial and trading crises. In 1391–92 the conflict between town and country, together with urban disturbances, brought about the disappearance of rich Jewish communities, above all in Majorca, but also in Gerona and Barcelona. And while production declined, the public debt rose. The failure of the Aragonese golden florin, the devaluation of the money of account in terms of the Barcelona silver groat (*croat*) bore witness to a weakening economy.

So it happened that the reign of Peter the Ceremonious (1334–87) was glorious but debilitating for the Crown of Aragon; in that of John I (1387–96), brilliant but disturbed, it is difficult to distinguish cultural interests, scientific and geographic curiosity from a craving for useless luxury and the occult arts. Lastly, that of Martin "l'humà" (or, the "humanist") was stamped by the bitter conflict with Sardinia. Genoa and piracy reigned in the Mediterranean, and death struck to the very heart of the royal family.

In 1410, the death of Martin occasioned a political crisis, since he had left no direct heir. Two years of interregnum led legally and in appearance peaceably to a settlement by arbitration, the "Compromise of Caspe" (1412). But it was a Castilian prince, Ferdinand of Antequera, who inherited the Aragonese sceptre. This ended the efficient collaboration between sovereign and Catalan bourgeoisie, and foreshadowed the decadence of Barcelona; it also symbolised a reversal of the equilibrium between the forces of continental and Mediterranean Spain.

Even if the apogee of Barcelona banking and commerce is located between 1420 and 1435, the Catalan economy nevertheless gradually lost its solid backing in population and production. Alfonso V, in leaving Spain for Naples, was ruined by an excessively broad foreign policy, penalised by failures at sea (Ponça, 1435) and by the rupture between Barcelona and the East. By mid-century the crisis was evident in Barcelona—between 1333 and 1450 foreign trade there had declined fivefold. Meanwhile the agrarian conflict had begun

again and two political parties confronted one another: the "Biga",
the party of the *rentiers* and the mercantile oligarchy of the importers
of goods, and the "Busca", the party of the artisans and craftsmen,
producers, exporters, partisans of monetary devaluation and protective tariffs. The King brought the Busca into the "Consell de Cent"
and angled social reforms in favour of the *remença* peasants. This
brought about a split between the Catalan oligarchy and the monarchy, which ravaged the reign of John II. During ten years of civil
war (1462–72) the Catalan prelates, noble lords and bourgeoisie
sought in vain for a monarch to their liking while John II found his
support in the bands of rebel peasants in eastern Catalonia. A great
politician, he was able to ingratiate himself with the defeated classes
and to prepare for his son, the future Ferdinand the Catholic, a
Castilian marriage, the key to Spanish unity. But the Catalan princi-
pality was exhausted by the crisis. Around 1484, when the Inquisition
was set up in Barcelona and expelled the converted Jews, the city
held less than 20,000 inhabitants. Ferdinand set about the work of
reorganisation and through the settlement of the agrarian conflict
("Sentencia de Guadalupe", 1486) managed to create in Catalonia
a strong and free, but numerically small, rural peasantry. However,
the demographic weakness and the ruin of the leading cities prevented the old Catalano-Aragonese states from conducting a policy
of their own in spite of the continuing possession of prerogatives
and institutions of government.

(b) *The vitality and triumph of Castile*

On the other hand, and often despite appearances, Castile laid the
foundations of her future leading role during the fifteenth century.
True, seen from without, the county appeared the victim of
anarchy. John II of Castile (1406–54) was a sophisticated weakling;
Henry IV, his son (1454–74) a sexual deviant in a court of eccentric
moral habits. But the court is not the kingdom, and through those
long reigns the kingdom had steadied and in truth asserted itself.

As for population, the Great Plague had seriously affected Castile,
but the consequences were less persistent than on the Mediterranean

coast. From 1400 to 1410 expeditions against Granada and Africa suggest a renewal of Castilian expansion, and during the internecine strife there was no lack of manpower in royal armies or urban militias. The so-called Quintanilla census taken in the reign of the "Catholic Kings" may not be acceptable (it assessed Castile at $7\frac{1}{2}$ million inhabitants) but it does appear that from the fifteenth century the balance of density was highly favourable to Castile and very unfavourable to the Mediterranean regions (in contrast to that of the thirteenth century and the present day).

In respect of the economy, the first major privileges granted to the "Mesta", the guild of transhumance cattle and sheep herders, were nearly contemporary to the Great Plague (1347). Those two events contributed at the same time to the extension of pasture over the mesetas (later to become excessive), which was to secure for Spain in a then impoverished Europe the highest possible production in terms of international economic values. The circulation of transhumance herds, voluntarily freed from the classic obstacles to commerce, increased internal Castilian trade and favoured the growth of fairs like that of Medina del Campo, already active from the beginning of the fifteenth century. This was reorganised in 1485 and soon after fairs developed in Villalón, Valladolid and Medina de Ríoseco. The "Consulates" of Burgos (1494) and Bilbao (1511), looking beyond the borders of Castile, ensured the export of merino wool, which led to Spanish merchants playing a preponderant role in markets like Bruges, Nantes, London and La Rochelle.

Castile possessed from then onwards two active maritime sectors, Andalusia and Cantabria, whose prosperity was interdependent. Between 1460 and 1470 the college of Basque pilots was founded in Cadiz, a source of great Atlantic navigators. Relations with Moorish Africa, either in rivalry or in agreement with Portugal, were both belligerent and commercial. Official and private expeditions carried over into African territory the work of the Reconquest, in search of that African gold so treasured in the second half of the fifteenth century, when precious metals appreciated considerably in value. The switch of military and mercantile manpower, first from the East towards the Western Mediterranean, and then towards West

Africa and the "Islands", was to end up by assembling about the Catholic Kings at the foot of a besieged Granada around 1480, a host of Italians, Spaniards from the Levant and converted Jews as well as military leaders and a multitude of indigent nobles in search of adventure.

In this context of economic, military and demographic expansion the middle classes played once again an important part, as in the heyday of the Reconquest. The lower nobility, the middle class clergy and the urban militias reacted vigorously in face of the disturbances between the barons and the throne (at its height between 1350 and 1450) and material and moral confusion at Court.

It was these same middle classes who supported a premature move to authoritarianism under a minister of John II, Alvaro de Luna (1445–53). The existence of Moorish and Jewish elements in the Court contributed to the popular success of sermons upholding the unity of the Faith and the pride of the *cristiano viejo*. One woman benefited from the expression of these emotions—Isabel, sister of Henry IV, who aspired to the succession. Public opinion preferred her to Joan, daughter of the King, who was universally considered as illegitimate.

Isabel stood for royal authority over against aristocratic disorder, morality against degenerate behaviour and the spirit of the reconquering race against Moor and Jew. In 1474, on the death of Henry IV, Isabel stood for something more—she foreshadowed Spanish unity, since she had married five years ago the heir to the Aragonese throne. It is true that at that time the King of Portugal sought the hand of Joan, the other heiress. It was a decisive moment. On which flank was the major act of Spanish history to be played? On the east or on the west? The future destiny of Spain gradually came to light over a ten-year struggle (1469–79). Modern Spain was to unite the traditions of Castile of the Reconquest to the Mediterranean ambitions of Aragon, and in the great emergent colonial enterprise, Portugal was to create an empire apart.

The triumph of Castile was even more decisive. The disappearance of Catalonia as a power, the commercial decline of the Mediterranean, the Castilian background of Ferdinand and the genius of

Isabel did not lead to the Levant playing the part in a unified Spain that a developing Portugal would have had if the cause of Joan had been victorious. From now on the militarist and pastoral spirit of the meseta, the spirit of the Reconquest, was to guide the history of Spain. In the make-up of modern Spain (and particularly in future colonial enterprise) what dominated the form of life and the manner of thought was the heritage of that prolonged medieval struggle and a territorial and religious concept of expansion, rather than commercial or economic ambition. To this prolongation of the Castilian medieval spirit of the Reconquest—so profoundly opposed to the emerging forms of capitalism—Spanish power at its peak was to owe its originality, its grandeur and, without a doubt, some of its shortcomings.

CHAPTER 3

THE MAIN LINES OF THE PAST: MODERN TIMES

1479–1598, three reigns and a little more than a century—this period was sufficient to allow Spain to achieve one of the most striking successes recorded by history. Too rapid, indeed, to be solidly grounded and followed as it was by a serious decline, it left to the nation an understandable feeling of pride (still perceptible in the spirit of contemporary politics) at having been not only a considerable power, but also the first nation in date and importance amongst those who founded vast colonial empires.

I. POLITICAL STRUCTURE

1. The strength and weaknesses of union

The marriage and happy understanding of the Catholic Kings made certain one fundamental event, the union of Aragon and Castile. In 1492 they took Granada; in 1515, one year before his death, Ferdinand dealt a decisive blow in Navarre. Abroad, his title was inevitably "King of Spain". It must be added that the west was not forgotten; it was not their fault if the two Portuguese marriages of their daughter only produced one heir who died young. But Charles V married a Portuguese infanta and Philip II was able to unite under his sceptre the whole Peninsula together with the two greatest empires in the world. The year 1580 marks the climax of Peninsular history.

But make no mistake about it, it was a fragile creation. Throughout the years 1497 to 1580 Portugal had by her conquests acquired an individuality of her own, and one of the first consequences of this union with Castile was precisely the loss of these possessions. That is why in 1640 Portugal rebelled. Could Spanish unity properly speaking offer any better guarantees?

In fact, it would have been difficult for the Catholic Kings to have wiped out during the twenty-five years of their reign all the centrifugal tendencies of past years. In the marriage bond Castile had insisted on underlining her rights: "Tanto monta, monta tanto Isabel como Fernando", and she had reserved for herself, at least in intention, the benefits of discovery: "A Castilla y a Leon, nuevo mundo dio Colón". At the death of the Queen, the Castilian nobility expelled Ferdinand, and it was only the madness of his daughter that brought him back as Regent. Aragon had kept her old administrative structure—in reality a federation of states in which Catalonia, the Balearics, and Valencia preserved with zeal their *fueros*, their "Corts", their customs barriers, their coinage, their measurements and their exchequer. Even when there was only a single sovereign, Charles I of Spain or the Emperor Charles V, viceroys were of necessity maintained in the old capital cities. The old kingdoms would not willingly accept "foreign" administrators and soldiers, that is to say, from Castile. For such a spirit to exist in harmony with the concept of unity, the central power would have had to exert only modest pressure and maintain a reputation beyond reproach. This was effected under Charles V and partially under Philip II, but they neither took advantage of it to undermine the old institutions, nor to exert control over them. Spain did not have its Richelieu or its Louis XIV at the proper moment. When Philip II first tried to interfere, Aragon brusquely reminded him of her ancient privileges. The first energetic attempt at centralisation was made in the seventeenth century by Olivares when the economic and military forces of the centre were already ebbing away. It was too late to be brutal— Portugal rose up and Catalonia offered herself to France.

The year 1640, in virtue of this double event, throws into relief one of the defects of the Spanish structure. No organic unity between the constituent parts could be achieved once decline had sowed the seeds of discontent; the memory of a glorious medieval independence was to return at intervals in future years.

2. RELIGIOUS UNITY; PROFIT AND LOSS

In point of fact the Catholic Kings had primarily directed their attention to another danger—the mingling of faiths, customs and race. This mixture, which had endowed Spain in the thirteenth century with a subtle complexity, gave way gradually to a passion for unity, a religious exclusiveness which was to characterise the Spanish people from then on. Why and how did this occur? It is a long story, often excessively simplified, and which does not start with the Catholic Kings.

When they ascended to the throne, the influence of the Jews at high level and the more modest labour of the Moorish artisan and peasant at low level in the service of Christian nobles had already inflamed the jealousy of the popular classes of Christian descent for more than a century and a half. Pride of race, of *limpieza de sangre* amongst the victors of the Reconquest, counterbalanced the fear of a too evident material superiority amongst the vanquished. The Church feared for the Faith in the midst of menacing heresies, and most of all in Spain, pervaded with the Jewish and Moorish spirit. The upper clergy placed reliance on public debate, but the monks, nearer to the people, pressed for forced conversion *en masse*. From the outbursts of 1348 following the Plague, to the pogroms of 1391 which tore apart the Levant, to the preaching of St. Vincent Ferrer, there stretch a series of popular revolts and campaigns for conversion. Loyal measures to protect and maintain order only closed the ranks of the various groups, and mass conversion created the *cristianos nuevos*, impenitent and mistrusted.

The reign of the Catholic Kings in the history of religious unity is therefore not the moment of origin, but the moment of crisis and choice. In 1478 the Spanish Inquisition was set up and directed primarily at the suspect Jewish converts (*conversos*); in 1492 the Jews were expelled *en masse*; in 1499 Cisneros launched a savage campaign of conversion in Granada; in 1502 he ejected the non-converted from the domains of Castile.

The problem, however, was not resolved. Charles V ran across it again in Valencia and the Balearics, as part of the popular revolt called the "Germanías". In 1525–26 he attempted to suppress throughout all Spain the very memory of the customs and the language of the Infidels. It was all in vain; the "Moriscos" could not be assimilated. Their habits of life and thought, their interests, their organisation (they made collective offers of money to the throne) drew them together as much as their ancient religion. They were suspected of collusion with the Barbary pirates and France. This "national minority" was attacked with well-known weapons: learned disputes, propaganda, separation of children and parents, police repression, confiscation of goods. The Inquisition was no more and no less punctilious in this repression than it was elsewhere and, despite all this, a terrible war continued to flame through the Andalusian south. The end is well known; under Philip III the conviction that a wholesale expulsion was necessary won through, and this took place between 1609 and 1611—a grave material loss to the country—but bringing this time internal unity.

This grave issue crossed with another. The intermingling in the mind of the Spaniards of certain philosophies rendered them particularly susceptible to deformations of the Faith. "Illuminism", Erasmianism, the audacity of certain religious reformers like Valdés and Servet, prove that the Peninsula had not escaped revolutionary trends in the Faith (indeed, perhaps the reverse). The reaction, however, was sharp. The populace and the lower clergy affected in matters of heterodoxy the same violent attitudes manifested towards Jew and Moor, and with the various rulers (particularly Philip II) the idea gained credence that Catholic orthodoxy was tantamount to national unity. And the right weapon was already to hand; the king only had to continue to support the Inquisition for it to stamp out, around 1535, the vigorous growth of Erasmianism, and later, under Philip II, all manifestations of Protestantism. At the end of the sixteenth century, the spirit of conformity triumphed over the spirit of heterogeneity inherited from the medieval period, and over the subsequent trend to religious diversity in the modern world.

How may we estimate the result? It is still an object of active, often acrid controversy. There are Spaniards who see in this religious exclusiveness the basis of all their past greatness; others trace back to it the root of national decline. They both forget to distinguish between two moments. The confluence of popular sentiment, ecclesiastical ideology, and political inclination in favour of religious unity on the threshold of the sixteenth century expressed without doubt some inner compulsion. But for Isabel, religious belief did not exclude prudence; Ferdinand's cruelty was not that of a fanatic, and Cisneros, the pitiless enemy of religious dissidence, was also—through his monastic reform, his University of Alcalá, his Polyglot Bible—a great artisan of Catholic reform. The reign of the Catholic Kings foreshadowed a century of triumph. If Spain was able to assimilate Charles V, it was because the ground had already been well prepared. If she conquered the universe and preached the gospel to it, led the Counter Reformation in deed and spirit, it was thanks to the moral accord created in the late fifteenth century that she was able to live through those celebrated years.

But the psychological process unlocked by the passion for unity gave rise to other results. The world surrounding Spain was changing, and she did not change. Religious conformity was in part responsible, striking at one extreme Jewish financial enterprise and at the other the agricultural vitality of the Moors in the Levant or Andalusia. The triumph of the *cristiano viejo* implied a certain contempt for money-making, even for the production of goods, and a certain attraction to the caste system. In mid-sixteenth century, the guilds began to oblige their members to prove their *limpieza de sangre*—a poor apprenticeship for entry into the capitalist age. On the other hand, the place assumed by the Church in society did not favour production or the circulation of money; the increase in the number of clergy, of charitable institutions, maintained the unproductive classes in a state of economic stagnation; the confiscations of the Inquisition, the gifts made to religious corporations, increased the amount of land held in mortmain. Finally, the finances of the State were to be ruined by the vain pursuit of hegemony in the spiritual world. Spain, whom the discovery of America could well have placed in the front rank of the modern economic world, did not achieve this position. All of this derives in great part from her religious psychology, blended with economic and racial elements inherited from the Lower Middle Ages. This debit element must not be left out in striking a balance on the issue of enforced spiritual unity; it foreshadows the "decline" and the attendant difficulties—still evident at the present time—which would have to be met by any movement for regeneration.

3. THE MODERN STATE

In the political sphere, the Catholic Kings had crushed the turbulence of the great nobles and begun to domesticate them; they had started to channel the adventurous spirit of the lesser nobility towards the army, taken over control of the Military Orders, and converted the local forces of order, the "Hermandades", into state police. They had introduced their *corregidores* into the major municipalities, been sparing in the convocation of the Cortes (no meetings between 1480 and 1497), and turned the *procurador* of these assemblies into a type of civil servant. On the other hand, they had founded at the centre a series of "councils" (of Castile, Aragon, Finance, the Indies), starting-points for a celebrated bureaucracy; for the administration of justice they created a *cancillería* (chancellery) and *audiencias* (provincial high courts). Their monetary reforms, their grants to the "Mesta", their intervention in the war of liberation of the Catalan peasants, reveal their economic and social preoccupations. In every field they left their mark.

Charles V, nevertheless, ran into one last spasm of medieval practice when he crushed at Villalar (1521) the "Comunidades" of various Castilian towns drawn up against him. From then on the future of absolutism was assured. The foundation of the *grandeza* and the *títulos* of Spain immobilised the aristocratic hierarchy, while in the Cortes the *procuradores* of the towns henceforward deliberated alone. Above all, the international prestige of Charles, and his sincere identification with Spain did more than previous measures to ensure the authority of royal power.

Philip II pushed to an extreme this preoccupation with absolute authority. He established first at Madrid and then in the palace monastery of the Escorial the vital centre of Empire. The thorough

Hispanisation of his power was such as to make it intolerable to certain of his possessions, and his scruples slowed down further an already clumsy bureaucratic machine. Secretariats, councils, *alcaldías, cancellerías, audiencias*, were costly to the administrators and ruinous for the administrated. Castile, less protected than the other old autonomous states, was crushed by taxation, and progressively sterilised by bureaucracy and corruption. Under Philip II's successors, the grand system of the modern Spanish state, too hurriedly raised up, became soon nothing more than a façade, still imposing, but masking a singularly dilapidated edifice.

4. Sovereignty abroad

It was some time before the "redoubtable infantry of the Spanish army" melted away at Rocroi (1643). This instrument was also forged in the reign of the Catholic Kings under "el gran Capitán", Gonzalo de Córdoba, who discerned the latent possibilities of manpower and military temper in the *hidalgo* class.

The origins of Spanish expansion are common knowledge. The dynastic policy of the Catholic Kings, and several chance events brought to rest upon the brow of a single heir, Charles of Ghent, Aragon and her Italian and Mediterranean interests, Castile and her first colonial conquests, the House of Burgundy, Austria and finally the Holy Roman Empire. The facts of general history are so well known that one merely needs to point out their significance for the future of Spain. On the one hand they drew together Spanish policy and the concept of Empire, on the other they caused her forces to be dispersed and led her to material decay.

It is not surprising that Charles V, surveying the extent of his imperial possessions, should have been inspired by the Ghibelline dream of unity. This inspiration would inevitably be influenced by Spanish tradition and the medieval spirit of her evangelising wars, not to mention the juristic and theological theses of her universities. But fully to understand what forces Charles expended in the service of this dream (forces less powerful than he believed he possessed), one has only to compare the brilliant and youthful victor of Pavia with the anxious and weary victor of Mühlberg and finally with the recluse of Yuste. His fatigue is the fatigue of the Spanish people—a few tens of thousands of fine Spanish soldiers is not much in exchange for world dominion. But the mercenaries had to be paid for, as well as the imperial voyages, the viceregal courts, the prestige of a sixteenth-century sovereign. What happened then to the modest budget *al modo de Castilla*, which the Cortes unceasingly brought up? The Crown was forced to resort to borrowing against the famous revenue of the Indies. In 1539 the bankers Fugger, Welser, Schatz and Spinola were owed a million ducats; in 1551, 6,800,000. From 1550 the income from the Indies was not available for years. The interest became extortionate: securities were taken up not only in the colonies, but in Spain itself—the *maestrazgos*, the mines of Almadén. When, in 1556, Charles V abdicated and split the Empire between his son and his brother, he thereby made confession of a double failure, political and financial. On the day of the great victory of St. Quentin which launched the reign of Philip II, the King displayed in his correspondence a veritable obsession with the problem of payment of salaries. The Spanish monarch, believed to be made of gold, was paralysed by poverty, and went bankrupt in 1557. The idea of imperial power was no longer viable—it was now the era of national politics.

However, Philip II would not admit it. He lent to his struggle with France the air of an anti-Protestant conflict. He defended the Mediterranean victoriously against the Turks. In this glorious decade —1571–80—opening with Lepanto and closing with the unification of the Peninsula, only two serious issues threatened the possessions of Philip II: one internal, the revolt of the Low Countries, the other external, the ambitious rise of England. Despite repressive severity, the rebellion of the "Beggars" could not be stamped out; in 1597 secession had to be admitted as a *fait accompli*. This was a serious moral blow, since it represented a victory for the Reformation. It was also a material blow, for it broke the economic solidarity of Castile and Flanders, foreshadowed the replacement of Lisbon and Seville by Amsterdam as a world *entrepôt*, and presaged the conquest by the Dutch of the Portuguese colonies. On the English side, the danger was even more far-reaching. Rivalry broke out between them under Elizabeth and lasted two decades, during which time Spain was stripped shred by shred. The Invincible Armada symbolised the Spanish desire to have done once and for all with this threat, and its failure in 1588 assured the nations in the North, up to then of mediocre strength, of a successful maritime future. This was a double triumph for Protestantism and capitalism, after which the world-wide structure of Spanish power could not last much longer.

II. ECONOMIC EXPANSION IN THE COLONIES

Nevertheless, the facet of Spanish expansion which continues to impress today has been its colonial development. No-one would deny here the mark of grandeur, and this has not failed to affect the latter-day Spanish conscience. History has offered few examples of such a degree of efficiency and despatch in an enterprise of colonisation and settlement. It should be remembered that the part played by chance—the "scientific error" of Columbus—cannot dim the fervour of those spontaneous enthusiasms out of which the Conquest emerged. Like a reprise of the Peninsular Reconquest, it was adumbrated in the Canary Islands around 1400, and developed parallel to the African expansion. The force of this thrust came from within the very populace of Spain—soldiers, sailors, clergy, settlers, and this despite the fact that she had recourse to foreigners like Columbus, Amerigo Vespucci, Magellan, all in their turn assimilated.

Two years after the deeds of Columbus, the Pope shared the world between Portugal and Spain. From 1495 to 1503 stretched an epoch of free trade and free navigation, backed up by powerful expeditions, like the second voyage of Columbus, or the fleet of Nicholas de Ovando (30 ships and 2500 men). It only needed ten years (1492–1502) to draw out the map not simply of the "Islands" (the Bahamas, the Caribbean archipelago with Cuba, Santo Domingo, Jamaica, Puerto Rico) but also of the continental shore from the thirty-fourth parallel south in Brazil to Labrador. In truth, it was often no more than reconnaissance, but already there lived in Haiti under Ovando "from ten to twelve thousand Spaniards, and amongst them many nobles and hidalgos". An important nucleus of the Empire was already in existence there and upon the Isthmus where Balboa saw the Pacific for the first time in 1513.

In the reign of Charles V the pace quickened, and the years 1519–22 saw unprecedented activity. Espinosa founded Panama: Las Casas attempted (in vain) peaceable colonisation; Cortés founded Villa Rica de Vera Cruz and transported his cavalry to Mexico where he crushed the great rebellion and was named royal lieutenant in New Spain. Exactly at the same time Magellan discovered the route to the Far East and his pilot Elcano received from Charles V armorial bearings with a globe and a device, "Primus circumdedisti me".

From 1523 to 1529 the exploration of Nicaragua was begun, starting from the South, and the exploration from the North of Guatemala and Honduras. On the southern continent, in Venezuela (ceded to the Welsers), in Peru, in the Plate River area, reconnaissance was carried out and points of penetration established, like Santa Marta and Cartagena de Indias. The dense character of the northern continent resisted deep penetration, but Alvar Núñez Cabeza de Vaca, in a fantastic expedition, crossed it from the Mississippi to California, while from the coast of Mexico Asia had already been reached.

The great territorial advances began again in 1531 with the brutal conquest of the Inca Empire. Almagro, separated from Pizarro, took over from Valdivia and struck out right to the southern cordillera of the Andes (1541, Santiago de Chile). In 1539 three reconnaissance columns which had set out from Santa Marta and Santa Ana del Coro joined up in the mesetas of the interior, and from the valley of Bogotá they descended together along the course of the Magdalena river to the Pacific. Meanwhile from Asunción, Irala organised the River Plate countries. In the North, Hernando de Soto reached present-day Georgia and Coronado explored Colorado up to the Arkansas river. Despite Portuguese competition López de Villalobos, having set out from New Spain, arrived in 1542 in the archipelago which he called "the Philippines". In fifty years the Spaniards had covered the coasts of the New World, east and west, to latitude eighty, crossed the cordilleras and the three altiplanos, reconnoitred the four great river basins and explored the Pacific. Wherever nature permitted a colony was planted, and thanks to the Negro slave trade the exploitation of Caribbean sugar got under way.

In Philip II's time the occupation of the southern territories expanded. Chile and the River Plate region were dotted with posts and foundations: Mendoza (1559), San Juan (1561), San Miguel de Tucumán (1565), Santa Fe (1573), Cordoba (1573), Buenos Aires (1580), Salta (1582), Corrientes (1588) and San Luis (1597). In 1580, through the Hispano-Portuguese union, the dominions of the Far East joined up with those in America. In 1564–65 the famous Basque priest–pilot Urdaneta managed the "return to the West" from Asia to the American coastline. Legazpí occupied Luzón and founded Manila; Mendaña, Sarmiento and Quirós discovered the Solomon Islands, Tahiti, the Marquesas, the New Hebrides, and Torres the strait that bears his name. In 1580 Spain possessed trading posts in Africa, India, the Sunda archipelago, the Moluccas, the Celebes and the Philippines; she was in contact with Japan and China, was considering intervention in Cambay and Siam. It is true that the Dutch rebels were already menacing these positions, and that in 1584 Raleigh offered Virginia to his queen. Spanish expansion had reached the limit and now confronted her enemies. But the mere list of advances over a hundred years cannot fail to astound. The names of the discoverers and conquistadors have not been overromanticised and their impetuous expeditions, their brilliant *coups*, their thirst for gold and their evangelising zeal truly constitute "the most extraordinary epic in human history".

Was it perhaps a simple adventure, stained in one place by avarice and in another ennobled by faith? The answer is no, because into it entered the whole creative spread of the sixteenth-century spirit, with its science, laws, politics, economics and empiricism.

It is clear that empiricism and private enterprise took first place. Spain, and no less Portugal, was the heir to Jewish and Moorish science, to Majorcan cartography, to the maritime experience of the Basque sailors; and their corporations, the "College" of Cadiz and the "University" of Triana foreshadowed the material power of the

Seville shipowners and the technical and scientific vitality of the
"Casa de Contratación" with its assemblies of cosmographers,
maestros de hacer cartas, capitanes de mar and *pilotos mayores,* authors of
artes de marear and *itinerarios.* The study of newly discovered territories—including their history and "human geography"—drew
equal attention. Fernando Colón is the *cosmógrafo cronista* of the
Indies, and apart from the excellent "voyages", "histories" and
"letters" known to all, it must be remembered that the preparation
of *catálogos* and *relaciones de viajes* figured amongst the official duties
of the discoverers, fixed by the "Ordenanzas de descubrimiento y
población". To this extent, then, colonisation was both voluntary
and planned.

In spite of the medieval character of certain "articles", of territorial concessions, or of the political organisation of the cities established, the spirit of the modern state presided over the colonisation.
The King, besides receiving a "fifth" of the income (regularly paid,
if not scrupulously calculated), preserved direct control of all conquests made. The contracts drawn up with Magellan and Loaysa are
very precise, and Pizarro took no steps without official orders. In
cases of necessity, even the most celebrated of the soldiers of fortune,
Columbus or Cortés, were called to order. Pedrarías executed Balboa
for his rebellion and the terrible quarrels between the conquistadors
(e.g. between Pizarro and Almagro) never gave rise to revolts against
the King before 1580. This legalistic preoccupation of theirs showed
itself in the curious custom of taking possession of lands in the presence of a public notary, and this was matched by the care with
which the monarchs established (from 1508) law courts and municipalities. This system, crowned by the viceroys and the Council of
the Indies, proved later to be clumsy and defective in function, but
it held sway for three centuries.

Is it possible to detect within this system a moral and political
concept of colonisation? This brings one to the famous controversy
between the "black legend" of "tyranny and cruelty perpetrated by
the Spaniards in the Western Indies", a legend broadcast by successive adversaries of Spain—English, French, Creoles of the era of
Independence—and on the other hand a counter-legend, much more

recent, tracing an idyllic picture of Christian colonisation by the Spaniards. It is imperative to distinguish between practice, no more brutal than any other type of colonisation, and theory, with laws of the most noble intent (often absent in more recent colonial enterprise). Since the "black legend" has been grounded above all on the passionate and one-sided denunciations of Bartolomé de las Casas, it has been easy to raise doubts about atrocities, for which history provides little concrete evidence. But the legal texts, the doctrinal pronouncements, are indisputably authentic. Uncritical denial of the *leyenda negra* is no more objective than its acceptance.

Today we know that all atrocities are possible. In a century when life was not worth much, in territory where isolation, hunger and fear compelled a show of force, the Spanish soldiers of fortune were doubtless guilty of the accusations made by Las Casas, confirmed even by those priests and chroniclers who censured his over-zealous passion. In the Caribbean, and particularly in Hispaniola, the conflict between gold prospectors and sugar-planters in search of local labour ended up, as is well known, in a veritable man-hunt, in the collective suicide of a race and its replacement by Negroes—and no-one disputes the existence of traffic in slaves.

When Columbus offered Indian prisoners to Isabel the Catholic as slaves, the Queen replied, "What powers has the Admiral received from me to deliver up *my subjects* to anyone?" This insistence by the Catholic Kings on ruling free subjects directly saved the Indians from legal slavery, for they were considered equal from the time of their conversion. This was, from 1500 on, the refrain that ran through the Laws of the Indies, but the constant need to revise them shows that there was a great gap between principle and application. The Conquest was inevitably exploited. Forced labour (*mitas*) was organised for the mines, based on local custom in the countries themselves, which presupposed a free offer of service. In the countryside, without extending or annulling the direct rule of the King over the natives, privileged colonists were "entrusted" with the "souls" of a certain number of inhabitants, so that the service given was justified by the protection afforded, that is, assurance of subsistence and the availability of Christian teaching. This was the *encomienda* system, which established a semi-colonial, semi-feudal relationship. Of course, in spite of its paternalistic character, there were abuses. Accusations were rife and the King took action, particularly in the "Nuevas Leyes" of 1542. Nevertheless, the beneficiaries of the system, with their strong organisation backed up by colonial groupings which did not hesitate to eject preachers from their cathedral pulpits, knew how to resist. As far as they were concerned, the King's will "se obedece, pero no se cumple".

This cannot belittle the political and moral controversy provoked by the system. It is an honour for a colonial power to have had a Las Casas, and not to have exiled or disgraced him. In mid-century the School of Salamanca, with Melchor Cano, Domingo de Soto, and Francisco de Vitoria, lifted the discussion from the humanitarian to the juridical plane of "human rights". Other theologians, like Sepúlveda, argued on the grounds of reason of state and the imperfection of human deeds. It also happened that pre-Columbian custom, and that of the Incas in particular, had an attraction for certain religious thinkers, and Indian settlements (*reducciones*) could take locally (as in the case of the Jesuits in Paraguay) the form of an authoritarian and theocratic village communalism.

At times the distance between theory and practice had fortunate results. The Inquisitorial censorship could not prevent American libraries stocking up with profane literature, nor the participation of the New World in the intellectual activity of the "Siglo de Oro". Even now the beauty of those colonial cities can astound us. It is more difficult to measure the real extent and penetration of linguistic Hispanisation and evangelism. The Indian substratum still persists to-day, for there was no systematic racial destruction, segregation or assimilation (the number of *mestizos* is enormous). From out of this complex base nations were to emerge.

It remains to consider the material results of the operation, in the Indies and at home. One inevitable conclusion is that the Spanish colonial enterprise was a decisive factor in the economic change from which the modern world emerged. This enterprise created the first "world market" and offered to European productive capacity increasingly cheap monetary cover. It will be seen later how this process ended up by excluding Spain from the development of capitalism. Her decline led men of the eighteenth and nineteenth centuries to believe that the achievement of the settlers was mediocre. Nevertheless, Humboldt had already shown that the major changes in the animal and vegetable worlds dated from the Spanish colonisation. From 1495 farm workers and artisans were persuaded to emigrate, even though the main attraction lay in gold and precious metals. Each convoy took on voluntarily grain and breeding stock—the source of American flocks and wheat fields. There was a legendary period of zealous cultivation, of pot-planting and the collection of seed. Even the most arrogant conquistadors, like Pizarro, sowed and planted, raised dykes and built mills. Thanks to the climate, certain successes were so rapid (particularly in the case of stock-rearing) that, despite the nearness of the mines, the price of meat and skins fell precipitately. Not everything succeeded; there were bankruptcies as well (e.g. silk, in competition with the Far East). But the sugar mills in the Caribbean and lower Mexico produced immense fortunes. The movement from America to Europe was no less important: even if one considers the maize and potato "revolutions" as being relatively late, it can still be said that the appearance of the New World transformed the agricultural horizon of Europe in the sixteenth century.

As for metals, one must remember the differences in time and place. There were areas like Paraguay so completely devoid of means of exchange that textiles and tools from Europe served as currency during almost the whole of the sixteenth century, while Mexico and Peru provided from 1550 onwards almost all the precious metals which were to flood Europe.

Chronologically one should not confuse the period in which the conquistadors, following the cadence of their fortunes, sent to Europe the gold of sacked palaces and plundered towns, with the time when, after the discovery of the Mexican seams and "the silver table with the feet of gold" in Peru, the settlers became first *entrepreneurs* thirsting after labour and afterwards skilful engineers.

In New Spain (Mexico) the mines and the great rural estates quarrelled over the Indian and *mestizo* labour force. In Peru where cultivated land was scarce and the peasantry tied to the land by ancestral custom, the emigration of the *mitayos* (Indians constrained to forced labour) had to be organised in order to assemble 150,000 miners and peons at 12,000 feet. Despite protective legislation and the efforts of certain viceroys, population declined in both cases, and this created in the late sixteenth and early seventeenth centuries a sudden rise in production costs of precious metal.

Meanwhile certain technical processes introduced by German specialists in the time of Charles V had been put into practice, but it was only towards 1554–57 that the mercury amalgam "revolution" brought about great savings in combustible material and the use of low grade minerals. Many Spaniards joined in these mining improvements, from Bartolomé de Medina, J. Capellín, F. de Velasco, Pérez de Vargas, Arfe, etc., to Alonso Barba, author of a famous treatise (1640).

Nevertheless the export of metals to Europe speeded up from 1503 to 1560. The first thirty-two years show a figure of 37·4 per cent of the total and the last ten 46·7 per cent, that is, a nominal value of 800 million maravedis a year. The decade 1591–1600 was to bring in 3000 million maravedis a year. This is, of course, the maximum; from 1600 the influx falls off, and towards 1630 the decline is very rapid. Moreover, while between 1521 and 1530 97 per cent of the bullion exports were in gold, between 1591 and 1600 87 per cent was in silver. The gold–silver exchange rate in Europe rose from 1:10 to 1:15.

While the Spanish colonisation revolutionised in this way the economy of two continents, let us now turn to its effect on the home country. This problem, a difficult one to resolve, has been dealt with in many ways and often over-hastily. For some, the "Indian gold" served in itself to ensure Spanish hegemony—for others it is the root cause of Spanish decadence. In the latter theory, Peninsular prosperity in the times of Charles V has been exaggerated; in the former, it has already been admitted that the geographical infrastructure and national psychology had always blocked productive efforts within the Peninsula. As before, one must establish distinctions in time and space. The fifteenth century saw an increase in population and

agriculture, a growing specialisation in wool production, a renaissance in internal trade, and a mounting share in international commerce, all of which prepared the external expansion of Castile. This
momentum owed nothing to the arrival of precious metals or
overseas colonisation in general. Quite the opposite, it evolved from
within—the epoch of the Catholic Kings was truly a creative epoch.

From 1503, the date of the promulgation of the decrees establishing the "Casa de Contratación" in Seville (modelled on Burgos and
aimed as much at the African as the West Indian traffic), it can be
said that Spain, and in Spain, Seville "passed from the limits to the
centre as it were of the world", in the words of Fray Tomás de
Mercado, a great historian of the fortunes and prosperity of that
city.

Doctrinaire liberals have severely criticised this Seville monopoly
(which was in no way a state monopoly like the Portuguese spice
market). In fact it was an efficient instrument clearly adapted to the
needs of the times. Seville was not only a hive of bureaucrats and
speculators; it was also a regional, national, colonial and finally a
world-wide port. The Andalusian landowner sold there his wines
and wheat, and every commercial enterprise in Europe of any
standing sent its representative.

It is true that the Genoese played a decisive part in the early stages
of the trade, and that at the end of the century foreign commerce
took control. But Spanish commerce did not suddenly disappear.
Up to 1560 Medina directed its merchandise and credits towards
both Lisbon and Seville, thus offsetting, even for Catalan cloth, the
loss of Far Eastern and Mediterranean markets.

Between 1532 and 1552, Seville banking—including the names of
Espinosa, Iñiguez, Lizarrazas, Negrón, Morga—"enfolded a world
and embraced more than an ocean" according to Fray Tomás de
Mercado. Unfortunately, added Fray Tomás, "its grasp was often
so weak that ruin followed on". But this is a fact belonging to the
second half of the sixteenth century.

Meanwhile it must be remembered that the "fabulous metal" from
the Indies had to be exchanged against something—mostly against
foreign products in increasing quantity. At first, however, it was

against grain, wheat, wine, oil, horses from Andalusia. The sudden requirements of the settlers, and then of those in Spain who shared in colonial benefits, explain the rise in prices of commodities over a wide range; wine went up most, and quicker than oil, while oil went up more than wheat. Out of this emerged the vineyards of Jerez and the olive plantations of Jaen. The expansion of silk production ensured the relative internal stability of Granada under Charles V; and as a result the question of the Moriscos could be settled by compromise. In Valencia, silk created what has been called "another India", while its vineyards and rice plantations flourished as well.

As for industry, one can hardly accept the figures attributed nostalgically by the *arbitristas* of the seventeenth century to the textile guilds of Seville, Toledo, Cuenca and Segovia. Nevertheless the peak of industrial production occurs indisputably in the reign of Charles V. Basque ore-smelting began at this very moment, and naval shipbuilding stripped the Valencian and Catalan coasts of trees. Urban growth, according to the so-called "Tomás González" census, reveals a remarkable industrial and commercial vigour together with a continuing demographic vitality; for, despite overseas emigration, there was no rural depopulation before 1565–75.

Although the historical reconstruction of this golden age of internal development is less advanced than that of the import of metals and Atlantic traffic (today well covered), one may locate in the period of Charles V the rounding-off of the spontaneous processes originating in that of the Catholic Kings, processes brusquely accelerated by the successes of the Discoveries. An assessment of the rhythm of development in Philip II's times can only be tentative. A report which should rank amongst the great mercantilist texts, that of Luis Ortiz, pointed out already in 1558 immediately after the failure of the Treasury the two major factors of future decline. These are: the imbalance between home and foreign prices, and state expenditure disbursed abroad. In what period, then, did these factors effectively bring about decline? It would of course be absurd to try and fix an exact date. Suffice it to indicate that from 1560 the rise in wages wiped out, for Spanish concerns, the advantages accruing from the price rise; the decline of Medina began, bankruptcies multiplied, and internal disturbances like the Morisco rebellion broke out.

But only after 1600, when the catastrophic plague of 1600 coincided with the relative decline of precious metal imports from the Indies, was the Spanish state forced to mint a base copper coin and pass from the "Golden (or at least the Silver) Age" to the "Age of Copper". At that point, the economic decadence became clear to all—and yet, despite this, the "Siglo de Oro"—the great intellectual movement of the times—still continued its course.

III. THE SPIRITUAL CLIMAX: THE "SIGLO DE ORO"

The Golden Age of Spanish civilisation was a gradual efflorescence, rather than a sudden radiance. The linguistic advances of the fifteenth century, the development of new literary genres, the refinements of plateresque art all foreshadowed it. Isabel called scholars together, encouraged the importation of text books and printing, renovated the University of Salamanca with its sixty-eight chairs; Cisneros founded Alcalá. The unfolding of the Spanish pre-Reformation, the humanism of Luis Vives are well known. The Counter Reformation was also led by high-minded scholars. Moreover, Roman Catholicism did not express its universality, like French classicism, in general formulae taken from antiquity—the medieval, national and popular note could always be traced in it. Vital and varied, the "Siglo de Oro" did not give utterance to the voice of a limited élite, but to the entire national sensibility.

One may begin with the line of mystics, prefaced by the first inventors of spiritual exercises—García de Cisneros, master of St. Ignatius, Ibáñez, confessors of St. Teresa, Alonso de Madrid, Juan de Avila, Pedro de Alcántara. At the lowest point of the line lies the gentle Fray Luis de León; at the highest, St. Teresa and St. John of the Cross, in whom the mystic life finds its perfect verbal expression.

The mystic tongue has its parallel in the arts. A Hispanised Greek composed in Toledo a synthesis of Byzantine sacred art, the last daring gestures of Tintoretto and Castilian grandeur. His art of pure form has made him one of the masters of modern painting. These shapes, however, have the power of revelation. When the curtain lifts on the *Burial of the Count of Orgaz*, the response of the celestial order to the terrestrial order, the upward thrust of the figures, the compactness of the portraiture, put the onlooker in touch with the interior life of a whole epoch. El Greco set the tone of the Siglo de Oro.

But these years of mysticism were not destitute of intellectual effort. Years ago (and perhaps with some exaggeration) Menéndez Pelayo rehabilitated the scholars of the Spanish Golden Age. Technicians, doctors, astronomers, botanists, philologists like Nebrija and Arias Montano, historians like Zurita or Mariana, follow one another from mid-fifteenth to mid-seventeenth century, reaching the maximum of vitality around 1580. In the field of economics, the "decadence" inspired the *arbitristas* with a thousand systems, and the price rise of the 1550's suggested already to Martín de Azpilcueta the quantitative theory of money.

The work of Suárez and Vitoria shared also a rational and intellectual quality. On the institution of sovereignty and human rights, they deduced from theological premisses a complete political doctrine upon which our present age still claims to draw, although the involved Latin of Suárez was probably ill-known to the publicists who so readily invoked him, a fact which is interesting in itself.

Literature itself was not exempt from intellectual subtlety. Above all in the seventeenth century, the passion and bitterness of Quevedo, the mysticism of Calderón and the poetic sensibility of Góngora took on a cerebral flavour—it is the very Spanish tradition of the conceit which extended even to Cervantes and St. Teresa.

Despite these speculations of a narrow élite, popular vitality was never stifled in art. Religious preaching, theatre, dance and song still preserved their medieval function. The spirituality of the age penetrated the widely read works of Luis de Granada, perhaps even more the polychromatic wood sculpture of Berruguete's disciples, often baroque in form, at times abruptly classical, and altars with their bleeding and tormented figures. The political structures of Suárez had their counterpart in naive but forceful psychological concepts of liberty, honour and the morality of the *cristiano viejo*, strong enough to react violently against tyranny and appeal to the sovereign over local injustice. The advent of such geniuses as Lope de Vega, Cervantes and Velazquez made possible the synthesis of past tradition with mystic fervour and intellectual force.

The theatre crystallised in the *auto sacramental*, the medieval mystery play. It also blended together, particularly with Lope, pure lyricism, a learned or conventional plot, doctrinal, religious, patriotic and often semi-revolutionary pronouncements, as in *Fuenteovejuna* or *Peribáñez* whose classical denouements uphold resistance to tyranny.

Cervantes possessed a more ordered genius, and his own life was a synthesis of the Spanish experience. A soldier at Lepanto, prisoner of the Moors freed by a *cofradía*, a more or less scrupulous servant of the crown, a faithful believer but not a conformist (for he was a true son of the Renaissance), he meditated upon his country and his times. Spiritual grandeur and nobility carried to an extreme, an inexhaustible fount of popular wisdom, a decaying fabric in an expanding world—these contrasts take on life in Quixote–Sancho, ideal and reality, individual and society. Since Cervantes possesses a genius for comedy, this makes us laugh, but as he has a gift for nuance, these contrasts are in effect complementary. As he has also a sense of the universal, the story becomes philosophical; but it remains also national and valid for its time. Don Quixote seeks medieval solutions to a modern world: crusade, adventure, the mystique of a world fashioned by the sword and embellished by the pen. Madness, it is true, but only because of the implicit anachronism. A symbol of Philip II, and of a Spain ineffective because ill-adapted, the armour of Don Quixote presents the same challenge to the bourgeois as Chaplin's jacket does to the worker: these are historical turning points and at the same time eternal works of art. Cervantes is the earliest and the subtlest of the *arbitristas*, those analysts of "decadence"; he lies at the heart of his nation's history.

A little later Velazquez presented a vision of Spain on the brink of the abyss. Like El Greco, this "pure" artist endowed with significance more or less conventional subjects in which appear, casually as it were, a landscape—the back-ground of the *sierra*: one last brilliant passage in history—the "Lances": a nation—the "Spinners", the "Drunkards", the blacksmiths and the beggars. All this, even today, can be appreciated by the most humble of Spaniards. Bacchus and Apollo chatting to an Andalusian peasant or a Castilian workman symbolise an art which draws invariably on two sources—the learned and the popular, imagination and reality. But one can detect an uneasiness here: degeneration at the top in the court portraits, degeneration at the bottom with the *pícaros* and the *bobos*. Here also a genius makes history manifest, not systematically, but with perfect lucidity.

Velazquez's Spain was still, however, an influential nation; it was the inspiration for France's *grand siècle*, and Castilian around 1650 was everywhere the language of civilisation. On the Isle of Pheasants (in the tapestry of Versailles) the august distinction of the Castilian court outshines the tasteless display of Louis XIV and his following. It was to be a long time before the *nouveaux riches* of England, the Low Countries and France herself could bring themselves to pardon Spain, while this country in turn adopted the *hauteur* of a gentleman fallen on evil times. The Siglo de Oro was, however, destined for a glorious rebirth. For the Spanish intellectual the grandeur of that past was the only compensation for the humiliations of the nineteenth century. The "generación de 98" distilled its essence, pressed out the last small drop from the *Quixote*, while the younger ones sought out Góngora and Quevedo. In the thought of twentieth-century Spain one can always detect the presence of the Siglo de Oro.

IV. IMPERIAL DECADENCE

Self-esteem went even further in the twentieth century; it denied the fact of "decadence". "No hay tal decadencia", said Azorín. The phenomenon, however, is quite indisputable; it is the interpretation that raises difficulties.

Population decline has been exaggerated, and as a consequence one is left with an insoluble statistical problem. There is no denying a fall in population, or the ruin of Castile, its industries, its stock-rearing, its commercial monopoly flouted by foreigners. The political *debâcle* on the other hand can be described and dated. Philip III, Philip IV and Charles II above all were sorry kings. If Olivares amongst the favourites had a certain nobility, the majority were mediocre schemers. Protocol, bribery, plot and intrigue stifled the efficiency of the central authority; and national unity suffered. The critical date, 1640, has already been mentioned. Portugal was lost; Catalonia was also in revolt, failed but tried again between 1700 and 1714. Beyond the frontiers, disintegration could not be halted. The Austrian alliance, aimed against men like Richelieu and Mazarin, was nothing but a source of failures. The treaties of 1648 mark the freedom of the United Provinces, the loss of Artois and the Flemish strong-points. The Treaty of the Pyrenees tore away Cerdagne and Roussillon from Spanish territory; the Franche–Comté and other fragments of the Flemish territories were lost in the struggle against Louis XIV. In the end, when the latter accepted the throne of Spain for his grandson, the cost of the war was back-breaking: the Catholic Low Countries, Luxemburg and several Italian possessions lost. Minorca, Gibraltar and favourable maritime agreements were amongst the trophies England won from her rival on the seas. The date 1713 lies at the lowest point of the curve. How far Spain had come since 1580!

This collapse made a great impression. Montesquieu pored over it as he did over the decline of Rome. Nevertheless, Spain's power was still a recent memory and foreign accounts were likely to be denounced as slander. "Factors of the decadence" and "black legend" often overlap, and the reaction to the "legend" was rarely objective. We do not yet possess a serious descriptive study of the continuous interaction between economic crisis and social decay, between the collective psychology inherited from a distant past and exclusively political responsibilities. Let us merely mention the problems involved.

The population fall is certain, but misinterpreted. Is this decline due to poverty, or is the poverty due to the decline? There does not appear to have been a decline before the last quarter of the sixteenth century. There are precise, but only partial, data on overseas emigration. The sum total is not striking, but what of the quality? It is 90 per cent male, and composed of the most active elements. The same problem arises over religious minorities. Was the expulsion of the Moriscos disastrous? To ascertain this, it must be realised that the majority of previous census returns did not include the Moriscos, and that the main problem is one of quality. One further important trend cannot be expressed in figures—the tendency of whole classes (younger sons ruined by primogeniture) to adopt demographically and economically sterile solutions to their future—"iglesia, mar, casa real". Other elements are even more difficult to classify—"students", vagabonds, beggars and servants whose picaresque way of life in no way favoured population or production.

The pure economic facts have been better analysed today: Hamilton and Carande have rounded out the old thesis of Häbler and Sötbeer on the effect of the precious metals on Spain. In the main, this was an inflationary phenomenon which after initially stimulating the economy, ruined productive capacity. The price rise began early in Spain (not exclusively attributable to gold and silver) and, if it at first made fortunes there, it brought in foreign elements, chased out good money with bad, encouraged contraband and unproductive economic activity. The change of situation, a fundamental issue, is poorly documented, and in any case it is difficult to believe that Spain would have put up so little resistance if her geography and her psychology had been different.

Were the Castilians ready to take on a leading role in the modern economy? Those who had followed up the discoveries for economic reasons were the Genoese, the Flemish, the Jews and the Aragonese followers of Ferdinand. But monopoly made the Conquest into a possession of *hidalgos* from Extremadura, stock-breeders of the Mesta and Seville civil servants. The profits were not "invested" in the capitalist sense of the term, and the fortunate emigrants dreamed of buying land, of building "castles" and of amassing treasure. The drama and the *Quixote* record this attitude in the peasant and the noble. A eulogy of Madrid construed her nobility in this way—all the cities work for Madrid, but she works for no-one. Recent pronouncements make a virtue out of Spain's incompatibility with capitalism, but this has condemned the country to inefficiency.

One last observation—might not this "decadence" be a crisis resulting from a change of equilibrium? From the fifteenth to the seventeenth centuries the central provinces had not only played a leading role, they had also a greater population and greater production, as well as economic and demographic superiority. Such a balance between the political force of the centre and its true vitality was an exceptional moment. After this remarkable success, geographical weaknesses and the heritage of the past led to a collapse which was felt over the whole country, so great that the coastal areas could not make good the losses of the fifteenth century. On the other hand, however, these areas (and the Levant in particular) suffered less from the general causes of the decadence: emigration, price rises, social *hidalguismo*, the weight of taxes and bureaucracy. Moreover, from the late sixteenth century they tended to inherit, on the Barcelona–Genoa axis, the Castile–Flanders currency flow, interrupted by the struggle against England and the Low Countries. In the eighteenth century the coastal areas turned out to be those most capable of recovery. From then onwards to the present day a new balance of forces emerged in which population and economic prosperity favoured the periphery. Is there any formula which can link this forceful activity with the persistent will to dominate manifest in Madrid? This was to be one of the most important issues of the coming epoch, the epoch of contemporary problems.

CHAPTER 4

THE MAIN CHARACTERISTICS OF CONTEMPORARY SPAIN

I. THE EIGHTEENTH CENTURY AND ENLIGHTENED DESPOTISM

The "contemporary history" of the Spanish people begins in effect with its first attempts to come to terms with the modern world. These attempts ran against social dogma, spiritual habits acquired during the Reconquest, consolidated in the Counter Reformation and fossilised during the "decadence": all of which created a conflict not yet ended, and of which the recent crises are only the latest episode. The first, and perhaps the most fertile, occurred in Spain of the Enlightenment.

1. RECOVERY IN THE EIGHTEENTH CENTURY; POPULATION AND ECONOMY

From 1700 to 1800 the population of Spain grew from six to eleven million, a considerable recovery in numbers. The factors of the decadence disappeared—gold and silver flowed into Europe through other channels than Spain. Foreign policy was limited to precise ends. Practically no more religious persecutions or expulsions took place. Even the balance of social categories changed to the benefit of the productive classes.

Did agriculture, a fundamental sector, change under these influences? It would be unwise to rely on Young's evidence. In eighteenth-century Catalonia there is concrete documentary proof of rural prosperity: in Castile the movement on behalf of agriculture against the stock-breeders' privileges is not an insignificant token of change. Everywhere, there were signs of activity, reclamation of land, "resettlement", creation of new villages—major works began again. Commercial activity is even more striking. In every Spanish port, the exchange figures rose. Around a revived Barcelona little ports equipped commercial fleets; from coastal and Mediterranean trade, they moved into traffic with America.

This is the greatest gain of the century. In order to acquire that right, the trading companies of the various ports accomplished more than the influence of theory at ministerial level ever could have done. The "Royal Guipuzcoan Company of Caracas" (1728) controlled the cocoa trade. There were two successive "Philippine" companies, and a Barcelona company for the West Indies. In 1778 free trade became general. Cadiz, deprived of the monopoly inherited from Seville, nevertheless maintained its prosperity. South America itself prospered under the sway of her great viceroys—Amat, O'Higgins, the Gálvez's and Cevallos. Barcelona merchants suggested types of colonial agreement to encourage industry. A great minister, the Conde de Aranda, laid down a federal plan in anticipation of the movement for colonial freedom which he expected to grow out of the North American example. Thus a political empire yielded to the concept of economic exploitation. Despite the imperfections of monopoly control and foreign smuggling, the eighteenth century is for Spain a great colonial century—a fact which is often forgotten.

Capital growth, import of raw material, rising population: eighteenth-century Spain at last began to industrialise, prodded on moreover by a mercantilist tradition which preached import reductions and "popular education" (that is, technical and craft education). Beside the Crown factories for luxury items, industries expanded wherever capital could be found. In Catalonia cotton replaced wool and technical innovations followed closely those in England. A commercial trading group made their express purpose the exploitation of American cotton plantations, in all a miniature "industrial revolution" which would be surprising if it were not related to two major phenomena of the century—the population increase and the revision of colonial relations. Would Spain get off to a good start in the industrial age? It was almost for an instant believable.

2. THE POLITICAL RECOVERY

From 1717 Alberoni had taken a strong line. Dynastic policies restored Spanish influence in Italy. In 1739 the Spanish navy broke a vigorous English assault. The 1761 pact with France brought with it the disillusion of the treaty of Paris, but the American war brought compensations. Minorca, Florida, and several colonial interests were recovered: the care lavished on the navy by two good ministers, Patiño, Ensenada, had borne fruit. Such achievements contributed to domestic unity. The Bourbon tradition inclined to centralisation and the Catalan rebellion of 1700 provided the opportunity for putting it into practice. Local privileges disappeared—the "regalism" of the jurists, manifested through the "Consejo de Castilla", replaced by *capitanerías* the *intendencias* and *audiencias*, those ancient organs of autonomy. Nevertheless, if these efforts succeeded, it was because a compromise had been reached with leading elements in the commercially active areas. By intelligent negotiation the Barcelona Chamber of Commerce obtained from Madrid the protection of the calico trade, the suppression of production levies, the revival of the "Consolat de Mar" and free trade with America. In the Basque countries, the enlightened élite founded the first "Sociedad económica de los amigos del país", later imitated all over Spain. The *escuela patriótica* in Vergara eulogised technology, industry, and the spirit of the *Encyclopedia*. From the provinces came the best statesmen of the Enlightened Despotism—cultured nobles like the Aragonese Aranda or the Asturian Jovellanos; *letrados* of humble birth like Floridablanca or Campomanes; administrators trained in Italy, Barcelona, Seville, like Patiño or La Ensenada.

Thus in reality the centre marshalled the vital forces of the rest of the country—unity was assured.

3. THE IDEOLOGY OF EIGHTEENTH-CENTURY SPAIN

Nevertheless there is a certain patriotic contempt amongst Spaniards for the eighteenth century as a "Frenchified" century. How far is this true? Cabarrús, who wanted "to wipe out in twenty years the errors of twenty centuries" is only one exception. On the other hand, the Spanish were by no means solidly behind Diego de Cádiz who thundered against this new heresy with a fury that recalls the fifteenth century. What is true is that a majority (*hidalgos*, peasants and the lower clergy) remained closed to the new ideology, the climate of opinion was "unresponsive" to it, while only a minority welcomed it, but with moderation and restraint. These "enlightened" classes in no way undermined royal authority; they laid siege to the material power of the clergy, drove out the Jesuits, made light of pious habits, but respected religion in principle. Moratín reminds one of Molière rather than Voltaire. Kings and their ministers let the declining Inquisition lay charges against highly placed individuals. Spiritual change, in effect, had its limits.

Nevertheless it did exist. The comprehensive world picture was breaking up; man's thoughts turned once again from heaven to earth. In the early years of the century Padre Feijóo undertook an examination of false beliefs, while the major works of the period dealt with social economy in a manner equally remote from the older political theology and the rationalism of "natural rights". In this sense, Spanish eighteenth-century thought is original. Campomanes, who, because of his attacks on the Mesta, is considered one of the founders of liberalism, re-edited the *arbitristas*, and based his ideas on education and industry on mercantilism; Capmany, well acquainted with new economic doctrine, nevertheless defended the guilds; agrarian private enterprise, antagonistic to the *Mesta* and entailed property, came up against not only the rural way of life, but also innovators like Aranda and Floridablanca. Respect for the past, for experience and a sense of history, infuse the intellectual production of eighteenth-century Spain with a sense of gravity and proportion, but on the other hand diminish that vigour and self-assurance which made France the century of revolution *par excellence*.

4. The limits of change in the eighteenth century

As we have said, the Spanish version of capitalism was in evidence by the end of the century—between 1787 and 1797 the total number of merchants and producers were up by 250,000 on the non-productive classes. This movement was encouraged by legislation against internal custom barriers, production levies, the import of machinery and red tape. Legislation also prevented the guilds imposing the test of *limpieza de sangre*, encouraged enclosure in agriculture, the sale of royal land, the disentailment of church property (in 1805 this disentailment affected as much as 6,400,000 *reales* of ecclesiastical revenue); ten years earlier there was a proposal that the aristocracy should give up the incomes from their entailed estates. In practice, however, these measures failed because of the extent of reform envisaged. In 1787 there were in Spain 17 "cities", 2358 *villas*, 8818 villages under nobiliary jurisdiction; 3 cities, 402 *villas*, 1280 villages under the "ecclesiastical patronage" of the Orders. Enormous riches divided the aristocracy from the poverty of the peasants. The figure of owners *and tenants* reached only 907,000 as against 947,000 *jornaleros*—the agrarian problem is already in evidence. This poverty explains the attachment of rural Spain to communal practices and charitable institutions. The figure for beggars was 150,000. All the ravages of the "decadence" had not disappeared. Charles III had fortunately limited nepotism, bribery and protocol, but provincial and colonial milieux, the lower clergy and the rural nobility remained attached to their ancient customs and their antique prerogatives. And the Spanish masses were still more receptive to the call of the fanatic reactionary than to the doctrines (rather pedantic it is true) of the writers of the "Enlightenment".

Thus any incidental crisis would be enough to put a stop to all the efforts of the century, and before the arrival of Napoleon the indifferent kingship of Charles IV prepared the way for such a one. Around 1790 Spain hesitated between revival and relapse, a dramatic moment caught yet again by a significant genius. The Aragonese Goya in his tapestries, his "Juegos" and his "Fiestas" portrayed the vitality and the *joie de vivre* of his century; the popular tastes of the *majas* and *manolas*, the *tonadillas* of Ramón de la Cruz and bull-fighting, now lifted for the first time to the level of an art. He was the successful satirist of the Inquisition, the portrait painter of the *afrancesados*, of Moratín, of the revolutionary ambassadors—a man, in short, of intellectual audacity. But he was also the painter of the *Communion of St. Joseph of Calasanz* (an echo of the mystics) and the devilish throngs of the black "Caprichos" (an echo of medieval times). Like Velazquez he is witness to the misery of the poor, the painter of beggars and slums: he is also witness to the spiritual poverty of the aristocracy. Across the faces of the *Family of Charles IV* is written the failure of another dynasty.

Napoleon's ill-disposed advisers spoke to him only of this failure. He neither weighed up the old instinctive vitality of the Spanish people nor the recent recovery in economic and intellectual values. But of these two elements which were to join forces against him— the will to resist and the will to change—which would win the battle for the nation's future? This is the drama of the Peninsular War.

II. THE PENINSULAR WAR

Charles IV had been an indifferent king. His favourite, Godoy, younger son of an Extremadura family whom the queen's influence had brought to power in 1792 at twenty-five, pursued a particularly disastrous foreign policy. He was neither capable of avoiding nor pursuing with zeal the struggle against the French Revolution. In Basle, Spain lost Santo Domingo, and the subsequent French alliance brought equally bad results. It cost Spain Trinidad, Louisiana, and led in 1805 to the Trafalgar disaster, which divided the colonies from the Hispanic world and left them to themselves—a significant date for the future.

Godoy would have dearly loved to turn about face, but Jena prevented it. He negotiated the division of Portugal which would have made him heir to its throne. But the French occupied strong points in Catalonia and Navarre at the same time as in Lisbon and Spanish independence was threatened. Opposition to his policy gathered strength—a conspiracy in court tried to remove the king in favour of his son Ferdinand, who showed his rather cowardly temperament by betraying his friends when it was discovered. However, public opinion held him to be a martyred hero. On 17 March 1808, at Aranjuez, while Murat was marching on Madrid and Godoy and Charles IV were thinking of flight, a rising toppled them both and proclaimed Ferdinand King. Murat refused to recognise him and mixing promises with threats he sent the royal family to solve their dispute at Bayonne in front of the Emperor. However, while pressure was being placed on the other members of the royal family to leave Spain, the Madrid mob, suddenly realising the meaning of these successive departures, hurled itself heroically against Murat's Mamelukes: this was the *dos de mayo* 1808—the Peninsular War had begun.

1. THE UPRISING AND ITS CHARACTER

What is interesting is the "style" of this insurrection, for it calls to mind more recent events. It is the first example of those collective outbursts of passion which shook the Spanish people again and again during the nineteenth and twentieth centuries, alternating with periods of depression and indifference, and always catching the government by surprise. Between 20 and 30 May 1808, Asturias, Aragon and Galicia refused obedience to those authorities who had collaborated with the French armies. In the early days of June, when the news had scarcely got about that Joseph had been named King, the French had already been defeated at El Bruch in Catalonia and harassed on the Guadalquivir. An organised plot, or a unanimous expression of feeling? It does not matter; the movement went deep and involved every province, a fact significant in itself. It penetrated to every social class, although the response varied. "Les honnêtes gens ne me sont pas plus fidèles que la canaille", said Joseph. Spain thus affirmed its solidarity and its worth as a single unit.

Nevertheless, the movement was not simply chauvinistic. It was a prolongation of the Aranjuez rising, the expression of an internal unease and a faith in the exiled Ferdinand, that fairy-tale prince. However, the hatreds and hopes of the Spaniards did not everywhere conceal the same image of the future. Some felt that the work of the eighteenth century should be resumed, and that Spain should follow France even while resisting her. Others saw in Ferdinand a patriarchal absolutism, a guarantee of tradition and the *fueros* of a medieval economy opposed to free enterprise, the close union of religion and politics. In short, "liberal", "Carlist", "Red" Spain and "Black" Spain existed already, joined against the enemy, but nevertheless in profound contradiction.

The average combatant was struggling against "atheistic" France, and once more the religious agitator triumphed. The *guerrillero* covered himself in pious images: the Virgin of "el Pilar" proclaimed that she did not want to be French. This national and religious feeling, however, was not simply passive conformity. The early insurgents took an evident pleasure in massacring the authorities. The parade of the victors of Bailén did not reassure the honest citizens of Madrid whom the former accused of passivity. Joseph compared the Spanish movement to the crisis of 1793 in France. It can be seen how this popular belligerence in the service of religion and tradition could easily turn against these two forces, and such was to be the history of the following century.

Paradoxically, the leadership of the masses fell to the tiny minority imbued with the spirit of the Enlightenment. The fact is that the number of politicians capable of rising above local quarrels was not great, and so the men of the Enlightened Despotism were sought out once again. The ancient Floridablanca, the conscientious Jovellanos were to preside the "Junta Central", the organ of resistance which had issued with difficulty from the provincial "Juntas". Then the Cortes met in Cadiz. Representation there was even more artificial. There had been no real elections; lawyers, intellectuals, businessmen, *americanos*, all mainly liberal, legislated in the name of Spain in beleaguered Cadiz—but without any contact with the mass of guerrillas. As Karl Marx said, the guerrillas acted without thinking and the Cortes thought without acting. This divorce between popular resistance and political authority was to remain characteristic of the nineteenth century. Another characteristic of this war was that Spain became once again *invertebrada*, returning to its *federalismo intuitivo*, as Menéndez y Pelayo would have it. The mayor of the village of Móstoles declared war directly against Napoleon; the Asturian Junta treated with England as one power to another whilst the constitution of the Junta Central led to curious federal proposals. In effect power was dissolving and this disturbed Napoleon: but Wellington, the author of a slow war of attrition, was more than scathing about the inefficiency of Spanish methods.

There is a certain hypocrisy in the English denunciation of the "inhumanity" of the war. The fact is that the Spaniards themselves carried on the struggle savagely, with cold steel, as if it were a personal affair, and justifiably enough if one bears French rapacity in mind! They also retained from the Middle Ages a taste for the spectacular and the macabre, a tendency to mass hysteria. But think of the nobility shown by Jovellanos, and the dignity of the Cortes, legislating for the future within the one single free square mile of Spanish territory! Think of the good humour, the display of wit in ballad and epigram. Spain was then being discovered by Europe, by the Romantics, by Stendhal. And the astounding success of this historical moment stilled in her for an instant the inferiority complex born of the period of decadence. But on the other hand, the country underwent no deeper transformation.

2. The failure of constructive effort

It would not have been illogical for "enlightened" Spaniards, authoritarian and cosmopolitan in their background, to have hoped from Napoleon the same despotism as from Charles III. Nevertheless, once the popular movement was unleashed, the number of convinced *afrancesados* was very small indeed. Both Napoleon and Joseph were disappointed, for they had hoped for more supporters. In effect Napoleon's confidential views justified Spanish mistrust. His reforms merely cloaked a desire for conquest and he paralysed the good intentions of his brother, while the generals through their depredations paralysed those of his administrators.

A Napoleonic movement for reform could not succeed, but a reforming movement *against* him might well do so. Several texts

from the insurgent Juntas expressed this idea, and this was the intention of the Cortes of Cadiz. From 1810 to 1812 the liberal
majority put the *serviles* of the Cortes (partisans of the *vieja España*)
on the defensive. As in the eighteenth century, Spanish liberalism
did not hesitate to defer to tradition and respect religious faith. But
it also attacked the material power of the Church, suppressed the
Inquisition and pressed for the "disentailment" of ecclesiastical
property. In political terms, its "Constitution" transposed the French
revolutionary principles: national sovereignty, separation of the
powers, the basic freedoms, a Chamber elected for two years by
indirect suffrage and with the duty to approve the Budget, a constitutional monarch with the right of veto, a uniform organisation of
boroughs and provinces. Most important, on 6 August 1811 *señorío*
jurisdictions were abolished with all their "exclusive, peculiar and
prohibitive" privileges.

This was the final stage of the century's evolution. The crisis
seemed to come to an end with the legal establishment of a new
social structure. But this was mere illusion. The separation of the
Cortes from the nation had its own consequences—its constitutional
work was ignored. Despite the reunion of the ordinary Cortes, the
people were mainly impressed by the defeat of the French and the
return of the King. Intrigue gathered force. The welcome given to
General Elío, an address by the "servile" deputies, popular acclaim
in Valencia and Madrid, persuaded Ferdinand in May 1813 to declare completely void the work done in Cadiz, and to include liberal
patriots in the *afrancesado* repression—*this is the collapse, not of a few
years' work, but of the achievement of a whole century.* The masses of
"España negra" triumphed over the enlightened minority. The war
had finally threatened the economic structure, and reactionary elements had endangered the juridical foundation which might have
adapted Spain to a century capitalist in its economy and liberal in
its politics. In Western Europe an anachronistic Spain continued on
its way.

III. THE NINETEENTH-CENTURY LABYRINTH

According to the approach taken, the political history of nine-teenth-century Spain is either picturesque or irksome, a mere sequence of plots, both comic and tragic. Let us give a brief resumé and then pick out a few of the main characteristics.

1. POLITICS IN THE NINETEENTH CENTURY (1814–1917)

(a) Ferdinand VII (1814–33)

His reign was marked by brutality and mediocrity in high places. The failure of reforms attempted in 1812 became more evident, and the Empire was conclusively lost.

From 1814 to 1820 a much despised *camarilla* of court flunkeys held power. Generals and guerrillas spent their time plotting. In South America General Morillo and his 20,000 men terrorised Bogotá, although this did not prevent the emancipation of Colombia.

A famous interval of three years runs from 1820 to 1823. In a continuously unsettled Cadiz a successful plot was carried out from within a colonial expeditionary force. Colonel Riego covered Andalusia proclaiming the 1812 Constitution. The moment his cause lost impetus, another revolt broke out in Galicia. On 10 May a frightened King accepted the Constitution. While the bourgeoisie welcomed the return of the "men of 1812", in Madrid the *exaltados* created trouble and the *moderados* fell. An absolutist, intransigent and "apostolic" regency was formed in Urgell. A frightened Europe was all the King needed, and in Verona Chateaubriand called for intervention. The "Cien mil hijos de San Luis" crossed Spain. The generals avoided combat and Ferdinand, re-established with all his powers, completely suppressed liberal legislation.

From 1823 to 1833 runs the "shameful decade", as liberal tradition calls it. Riego and his friends were executed: in 1825 the most popular of all *guerrilleros*, el Empecinado, was shot; in 1826 the Bazáns were executed, and in 1831 Torrijos and Mariana Pineda, guilty of embroidering a flag. Despite all this the fanatical *apostólicos*, still discontented, grouped into factions and put their faith in the succession of Don Carlos, the King's brother. However, in 1830 Ferdinand had a daughter by his third wife María Cristina. The partisans of Don Carlos invoked the Salic Law of the Bourbons, and in order to avoid disinheriting his daughter, Ferdinand had to make certain concessions to the liberals. Repression became less harsh; finances and the economy recovered. But after 1824 and the resounding defeat of Ayacucho, practically all hope of recovering the great South American colonies was lost.

(b) *The age of the pronunciamiento (1833–75)*

From 1833 to 1840 María Cristina was regent for her daughter Isabel II. But Don Carlos had been proclaimed King by his supporters. The first carlist war lasted seven years, covering principally the Navarrese, Catalan and Valencian uplands. Madrid was only threatened once in 1838. Nevertheless the Regent had her problems. Liberal despite herself, she tried to govern through the *moderados*. Opposition grew, and in 1835 an epidemic sparked off a popular rising against the monasteries. Martínez de la Rosa had to yield power to Toreno, then to the banker Mendizábal under whom anticlericalism flourished for a moment. In 1836 at La Granja junior officers imposed on the Regent the Constitution of Cadiz. She managed to replace this in 1837 by a more moderate one. In 1838 when "el abrazo de Vergara" between Espartero and the carlist Maroto appeared to have ended the war, the Regent believed she could exert her authority. But the *progresista* Espartero "pronounced" against her, and after her banishment, the "Duque de la Victoria" replaced her as Regent.

1840–43. The popularity of the new Regent was short. He governed with the help of a *camarilla*, shot the rebellious generals, and bombarded Barcelona after a rising. After that he was known simply as *el ayacucho* (an allusion to his rather inglorious role in the colonies). In 1843 unrest grew in the towns; the *moderados* (Narváez, Concha) returned from exile, and Espartero left for London, but not before bombarding Seville.

1843–54. Once Isabel was proclaimed of age, the *moderados* used her against the *progresistas*. González Bravo and then Narváez hammered out the weapons of authority—first the "Guardia Civil" in 1843 and in 1845 a Constitution very favourable to the executive power. In 1848 Narváez forestalled revolution by bloody repression; in 1847 the carlist guerrillas appeared once again.

The Queen's marriage raised an international problem which was resolved by providing her with an insignificant husband. But now the palace intrigues were the talk of the town. Other scandals followed—the success of the financier Salamanca, bribery under the minister Sartorius. Since Narváez had retired in 1851 in face of this array of doubtful personalities, the reaction came in the form of a pronunciamiento by *moderados* and *progresistas*, generals and politicians—this was the so-called *vicalvarada* of 1854 (after the battle of Vicálvaro) which starred a new general, O'Donnell, and brought back Espartero.

1854–68. Their duumvirate was short. Overwhelmed by popular agitation in Andalusia, they were eliminated one after the other by the Queen. From 1856 to 1868 Narváez and his *moderados* alternated with O'Donnell and his left-centre group (the "Unión liberal"). But the democratic parties were emerging; the republicans under Castelar and Salmerón, the federalists under Pi y Margall, while incidents abroad (Morocco, Chile, Mexico) brought two more generals, Serrano and Prim, onto the stage. The latter, in four years, attempted seven pronunciamientos in the *progresista* tradition. But the old authority was wasting away. Narváez and O'Donnell died in 1868. The Queen was universally considered as *insoportable* on account of her private life. González Bravo tried to repress the agitation and attracted the hatred of everyone. The Fleet, the garrisons, local *juntas* proclaimed universal suffrage and "the fundamental liberties". Serrano was put at the head of the movement and defeated the Queen's troops while she fled to France.

1868–75. Serrano and Prim, the provisional rulers, convoked the Cortes. Although a monarchical constitution was approved, this assembly was outstanding in character and very democratic. It was, however, difficult to find a king. And the day Amadeo, son of the

King of Italy, arrived, having accepted the throne, Prim was murdered, 30 December 1870. The King, left to himself, was exhausted by the difficult situation—the rivalry between Sagasta and Ruiz Zorrilla, the resumption of the carlist war and the social disturbances of the "International". He abdicated and a Republic was proclaimed (February 1873). The main tendency here was to federalism, the president being a Catalan Pi y Margall. But anarchist influence transformed federalism into *cantonalism* and a group of communes proclaimed their independence. Pi resigned rather than be forced to use repressive methods, while Salmerón refused to use the death penalty. With Castelar, who replaced him, an authoritarian and centralist Republic came to power. But it was too late. On 3 January 1874 General Pavía had the Cortes forcibly dissolved and a provisional dictatorship paved the way for the Restoration in favour of Alfonso XII, son of Isabel II. He arrived from England with an experienced tutor in his retinue—Cánovas del Castillo, the "liberal conservative".

(c) The Restoration (1875–1917)

We shall only take the Restoration here as far as 1917, a date which opens the series of contemporary crises. The period in general is characterised by the alternation in power (*turno político*) of the two major parties, conservative and liberal, flanked by two other parties theoretically in opposition, carlist and republican.

From 1875 to 1885, with the carlist war over, a skilful Constitution handed local power to the petty bosses or *caciques*, and national power alternately to the two parties. Cánovas was the central figure. In 1885 the King died prematurely; the Queen was expecting a son, and she took over the regency.

From 1885 to 1902, the parties signed a truce—here the controlling personality was the liberal Sagasta. The prudent dignity of María Cristina was well respected, but a disaster intervened. Repression failed against the independence movement in Cuba and the rebellion in the Philippines, whilst the intervention of the United States revealed to Spain her real weakness. This Imperial collapse in 1898 provoked outbursts from the intellectuals and in the vigorous provinces of Catalonia and the Basque country. The time had come for serious changes.

From 1902 to 1917 under Alfonso XIII the tension increased. The conservative Antonio Maura had a breadth of vision, but made enemies all round, while the liberal Moret merely engaged in short-term intrigues. The gravest problems were rooted in Catalonia—proletarian anarchism, intellectual and bourgeois regionalism. In 1906 the "Solidaritat Catalana" party presented itself at the elections: in 1909 the mobilisation of troops in Barcelona for Morocco triggered off the "Semana Trágica" which ended in the execution of Ferrer who was accused of being intellectually responsible. Maura was firmly rejected as a result, and this brought the liberal Canalejas into power. From 1910 to 1912, he tried manfully to resolve the Moroccan problem, limit the power of the clergy, offer to the Catalans partial autonomy in the form of the "Mancomunitat". But Canalejas fell in his turn victim to an anarchist. Then Romanones and García Prieto served turn about with Dato, Maura's rival in the conservative party. With the First World War supporters of Germany and of the allies (or the right and the left, authoritarians and liberals, exceptions aside) stood face to face. Neutrality was maintained, but the high cost of living and the increasingly important role of the industrial proletariat ended by provoking in 1917 a grave crisis, the first episode in the troubles of contemporary Spain.

2. POLITICAL LIFE IN NINETEENTH-CENTURY SPAIN

Tremulous and hesitant, Spanish political activity in the nineteenth century skated over the surface of society. In the twentieth century stakes were larger, the masses more directly involved; but old habits died hard, and it is useful to be able to identify them.

(a) *The monarchy*

The monarchy never took up the leadership which the country offered it in 1813. Ferdinand remained the petty intriguer of 1808, the tool of ill-chosen advisers, fearful and vengeful. María Cristina had quite different aptitudes, but, liberal through force of circumstance, she had to play double with her own supporters. A favourite target for carlist slander, she was in effect an easy subject for epigrams because of her marriage to the palace guard Muñoz (seven children had to be given titles and dowries). Isabel was worse, making and unmaking ministers "to the tempo of the rigadoon" and not without duplicity. Her private affairs gave the carlists and republicans even more opportunities for indignation and ridicule. It is true that a disappointing revolution made one appreciate the wisdom of Alfonso XII and the dignity of the second Regent; but all this hardly helped the monarchy to escape unscathed from the colonial disaster. Finally came Alfonso XIII, a stronger personality, who courted popularity with his youth, his irony and his rather theatrical Spanish *casticismo*. However, he put power above office, and "secrets" above obligations. From 1920 one fact was clear to the Spanish people: he had become, as his grandmother once was, *insoportable*.

Thus, while convinced royalists continued to be absorbed by the carlist issue the disputed branch never received from the masses that respect which provided a solid base for the monarchy in Sweden or England. In Spain, during the series of contemporary crises, it never became a useful symbol for the body politic.

(b) *Constitutions and representative government*

Nor did a democratic tradition take shape. The constitutions which roused enthusiasm (1812, 1869) were only briefly applied; others (1834, 1837, 1845, 1856) were enforced compromises. That of 1876 lasted longer, establishing universal suffrage in 1890 and remaining in force until 1923. But this parliamentarianism was never able to resolve the serious crises—in short, it did not represent the country.

It is not that representative government is contrary to the Spanish spirit. The Spanish intelligentsia has a very pronounced taste for legality and constitutional subtleties. Political oratory, whether it be the flowery phrases of Martínez de la Rosa or the vehemence of Castelar, inspired more enthusiasm than the ability to govern, and the wider public were no less impressed by the sayings of their parliamentary stars whose oratorical battles they followed with all the fascination of a drama.

The nineteenth century offers, it is true, more comedies than dramas—conspiracy, intrigue, sometimes bribery, although the great politicians were rarely tempted. Their supporters, however, often got their hands dirty. There were frequent municipal scandals in the big towns. During the Restoration the political "turnabout" implied ultimately the switch of personnel in administrative sinecures, so that public service became private profit. Politics was compared with cooking chops—each side wanted their turn in the gravy. The humorous writers of the time have repeatedly described the social figure of the *cesante*, a civil servant in enforced retirement spending his days in the Puerta del Sol until his own bunch got in again. In the provinces, the key political figure and ultimate beneficiary was the *cacique*, a small town representative or a village electoral agent who owed his position to family tradition or to the nature of his local role—in Andalusia, for instance, he farmed out work as the steward of the landowner. But elections of this type are meaningless—elections are effected without opposition, by fraud or by agreement, and the electorate exercises no control. The Cortes becomes a club for academic discussion on budgets or taxes. Authority of necessity becomes pure caprice. Caprice, to paraphrase the words of Unamuno, is the natural regime of the Spanish people, who temper it at the top by the pronunciamiento and at the bottom by anarchy—a boutade if you like, but it explains why even today the Spanish people look less to King or Parliament than to the Army or Revolution in the streets.

(c) *The pronunciamiento*

The absence of real foreign commitments, the irregularity of recruitment, the ignorance of the troops, long prevented Spain from having a citizen army. The officer had always counted more than the private, the special corps more than the ordinary unit. Nevertheless, it was no comic opera army. The events of 1808, the carlist war and colonial repression had forged and trained it above all for the home front. Without representing the spirit of the nation, the army was a force capable of enshrining a political creed. Periodically a well-known process took place. Exiles, secret societies, often foreign intrigue, obscurely encouraged by partisan opinion, and aware that legal channels had been closed by official pressure, elected a general, frequently a leader in exile, or at least in disgrace. The *coup* usually occurred at a port of embarkation or some remote locality. A manifesto was read to the troops, who abandoned their barracks. Arrests were carried out, commands changed, while express messengers and telegrams called on other garrisons, previously approached, to make a pronouncement in the same terms. Madrid usually declared the situation under control (this was often true since out of scores of failures only half a dozen pronunciamientos were successful). If the conspiracy was ripe, resistance was short, for a pronunciamiento never set off a civil war—that is until 1936, and this was the great change.

These were no comic opera plots either. Several dozen unfortunates were executed and the reprisals were drastic. For his opposition to the "golpe de los sargentos", General Quesada was assassinated, his fingers chopped off, taken to the "Cafe Nuevo" and used to ladle out the punch to his enemies.

Can any trend be detected in these savage struggles? Early in the century the young officers were forward-looking, liberals and Masons. Later it was the authoritarian leaders like Narváez who took over. However, the "people's general", the democrat or at least self-declared democrat, was probably a nineteenth-century type. The true watershed occurs around 1868–73. Faced with the revolutionary temper of the people and the new ideologies of the intellectuals, the army found itself moving more and more towards "order", moral and social order. However, the situation was never completely clear-cut. Habits and memories (particularly of freemasonry) made it still possible in 1930 to have a republican pronunciamiento, while the military rising in 1936 reminded many of the pattern of the *coup d'état* against an irresponsible government. But the illusion did not last, and from then on the position of the army in society has been clearly defined. It can be seen, therefore, in how many different ways the pronunciamiento could work in practice.

(d) Civil war and disturbances

The same applies to the recurrent and unpremeditated uprisings of the Spanish people. The carlist wars fall into this category—their psychology is that of the 1808 outburst. The Catholic, absolutist sermons of the clergy and local chiefs express the same demagoguery in close association with the defence of regional *fueros* and communal agrarian customs. Out of the three carlist strongholds (the Basque provinces, Navarre, Upper Catalonia) two support today a type of autonomous democracy. Is there any significance in this fact? In any case, the carlist wars are a portent of 1936—whole villages up in arms, incomprehensible hatred between families, intervention of the military and the clergy.

The Andalusian disturbances are quite different. Poverty and land hunger bring back age-old habits—the partitioning of estates, illegal timber-cutting, arson, massacres of *caciques* or police. These peasant revolts recur in 1856, 1861, 1873, 1876 and 1892, following on agitation which was attributed to "communism" after they had started up again in 1917–19.

The urban outbursts, on the other hand, preceded the organisation of parties and trade unions. In the violent urban eruptions of 1827, 1835, 1840–42, 1871–73 and 1909 all the contemporary trends can be recognised, often improperly ascribed to the "propaganda" which preceded them. From 1830 to 1840 individual outrages against society were common in Barcelona; in 1842 and 1873 one can distinguish a trend towards federalism and cantonalism; finally, and most important, from 1835 to 1909 runs an unbroken series of attacks against the clergy and religious orders, who were accused of being responsible for many things, often fantastic (like the Madrid cholera outbreak), and often true (favouring repression and counter-revolution). In the same way "Red Spain" was to turn against "Black Spain" with its anti-heretical campaigns and carlist wars.

To understand the years 1930–39 one cannot leave aside the urban *putsch*, the agrarian outburst, the alternation of parliamentary oratory and the *coup d'état*. In the twentieth century the germs of the struggle were more virulent—and this is because between 1814 and 1917 the basic problems grew more serious.

IV. THE BASIC PROBLEMS

1. DEMOGRAPHY AND ECONOMY

The weaknesses of nineteenth-century Spain were not the same as those of eighteenth-century decadence. They are not related to a population decline, but to the difficult problem of meeting a constant demographic rise. In fact, from about 11 million in 1808 the Spanish population reached 15·5 million in 1857, 18·5 in 1900 and 24 in 1935—a rapid increase for a poor country. In the twentieth century Spain arrived at a "critical density" which demanded a new technical and economic approach. The possible methods of adaptation (intensive agriculture, industrialisation, imperialist ventures) would demand capital, a spirit of enterprise and colonial bases— items which the country nearly acquired in the nineteenth but lost in the opening crisis of the twentieth century. The adaptation, when it occurred, was unsystematic. Agrarian Spain placed material, legal and psychological obstacles in the way of capitalism; industrial Spain, in order to live, needed to shelter behind a protectionism which soon weighed heavily on the rural majority. The problem was not grave as long as agricultural progress outstripped population increase. In the first third of the century the cultivated area rose from less than three to more than five million hectares—in 1829 Spain exported wheat. But the limits of this approach soon became obvious.

2. AGRICULTURAL PROBLEMS

(a) *Technical and economic issues*

Dry Spain (plateaux and river basins) has only practised one type of intensive agriculture—dry-farming, a natural response to the climate, but this meant spaced-out harvests and minimum returns. On top of this stock-breeding had been for ages a predominant occupation. When agriculture spread, the law of diminishing returns went quickly into operation; and finally after an increase due to fertiliser the limit for wheat turned out to be lower than nine quintals per hectare! It became absurd to break new ground, for in fact success had only been obtained (in Mediterranean crops) through high concentration, intensive cultivation and specialisation. To extend this to Aragon, to the south-east and to Andalusia irrigation was indispensable—and large-scale irrigation at that.

In this particular field, nineteenth-century capitalism failed. In one attempt to make the desert flower, the economic yield turned out to be long-term. The Urgell canal, built around 1860, wondrously transformed a whole area, but with such delays that the financial backers were seriously disappointed. Conversely, in the south-east, well populated and fertile, but with a less even climate, the major works (the Lorca basin, later "Riegos de Levante") have been remunerative, but simply because the water was auctioned; and this exploitation of water-shortage during drought ruined the peasant.

From these two types of failure certain conclusions were drawn. These favoured a state intervention capable of reviving on a national scale and by modern technology the old *comunidad hidráulica* through which the equitable distribution of free water was guaranteed once the costs were covered. This "irrigation policy" (real socialism in effect) had one apostle—Joaquín Costa, an Aragonese deputy with a muddled turn of phrase, but clearly the best brain which the '98 disaster served to stimulate. Unfortunately little research was done; the State was poor and local vested interests, bribery and corruption plagued the concession of tenders. For this reason the "Gasset plan" of 1902 failed (the engineers had proposed a dam on every gorge!). Despite this, irrigation policy became inseparable from any progressive proposals, the success of which would mean true revolution; but it was also to run up against the social situation.

(b) *Agrarian issues*

The agrarian system of the *ancien régime* had lasted into the twentieth century without giving place to any balanced solutions. Old habits weighed heavily—in Aragon, Andalusia and Extremadura the psychology of the seignorial regime lived on despite the disappearance of its legal system. In Galicia *censos* and *foros* were still imposed in the twentieth century on *minifundios* so small that they could hardly support a family. Even Catalonia, socially more settled, had its agrarian troubles. The old vine-growing contract of *rabassa morta* had bound the tenants to their land for centuries; but it was related to the life of the vine-stock and phylloxera had interfered with its effectiveness. A struggle for land then set federations of landowners against tenant unions (*rabassaires*) bringing crises in 1890, 1920 and 1934. Much of Catalan politics derived from this issue.

Finally, in the south, there was the *latifundio* problem. Nineteenth-century efforts on behalf of agrarian free enterprise brought no great success. The disentailment of property was, on the surface, one of the great events of the century. The sale of ecclesiastical property, the buying back of *censos* and annuities represented between 1821 and 1867 a sum of 2700 million pesetas. But the interruption of the policy (decrees of 1821, 1835, 1854, suspended in 1823, 1845, 1856), the poverty of the peasants and local customs, meant that the operation did not lead to the highly exploited large estates of the English or Prussian type, nor a satisfied peasantry like the French. The speculators in this affair created other *latifundios* in addition to the aristocratic ones. The agrarian structure did not change.

Thus at the beginning of the twentieth century, 10,000 families owned 50 per cent of the assessed lands, and 1 per cent of the landowners 42 per cent of the capital value of land. The maximum size of estates was not excessive—in Cadiz 30,000 hectares to every ten owners (it has been accepted that a *latifundio* may be defined as an estate over 250 hectares). Nor was it always a question of working barren land. In the Jerez vineyards, 3 per cent of the landowners possessed 67 per cent of the estimated wealth. The rich munici-palities (Carmona, Ecija, Utrera, Seville) held 45 to 81 per cent of their land in large estates. And even here the cultivation was *extensive*. Fallow land, hunting preserves, bull-breeding for the *corrida*, cork oak and olive plantations, dry-farming of wheat, this order of priorities was not based on the potentialities of Andalusia. The Medinaceli family devoted for years 15,000 out of 16,000 hectares of good land to the hunt and the Dukes of Alba let at 25 pesetas a *fanega* tracts of land sublet at 60 by their bailiffs. In this way capital was neither built up nor invested. An irrigated hectare would bring in twenty times more than one hectare of dry farming, but it would cost seven times as much as well as needing large capital invest-ment. Thus *latifundia* did not allow the development of intensive farming.

Seen in another way, the problem is a social one. The Andalusian peasantry is composed of *braceros*, day labourers who bring only their hands to the job. They earned, from 1900 to 1930, an average of 3 pesetas a day, with standoffs of between 100 and 150 days a year. The proletarian aspect of the peasantry is even clearer when one considers that they live in towns of 10 to 15,000 inhabitants, where they are contracted for seasonal work in the *cortijos*. The birth rate, however, is high and the emigration rate low. This means overpopu-lation, poverty and undernourishment. An apathetic race, it has been said. But this apathy has not been uninterrupted—there have been uprisings and outbreaks of violence. Now this is a phenomenon which applies precisely to a third of Spain, and to that part which was once its most beautiful garden. These millions of men who produce little and consume equally little are a dangerous dead-weight for the national economy as well as a cause of social im-balance. After having disregarded the problem for a long time, the Spanish authorities stepped up their research on the subject. How-ever, the Institute for Social Reform, founded in 1902, was simply a study unit. It only attempted reforms on an experi-mental scale and no overall plan was tackled before 1931, while around 1917 serious social uprisings took place once more in the south.

3. INDUSTRIALISATION AND EQUIPMENT

On the industrial side, Spain possessed several advantages—her mines and her labour. But she lacked heavy industry capital and markets for consumer industries. These two factors were to have grave consequences.

(a) *Mining production, general plant and heavy industry*

These either lagged behind or fell into foreign hands. The mines tripled the value of their output between 1830 and 1856, and then between 1860 and 1900. From 1864 to 1913 production rose: for iron ore, from 280,000 to 9,860,000 tons; for copper ore, from 213,000 to 2,268,000; for coal, from 387,000 to 3,700,000. But the weak Spanish companies did not fare well in their development. Foreign capital outstripped them (667 million pesetas against 605 in 1920). This was concentrated in large enterprises: Belgian (Real Asturiana de Minas); French (Peñarroya); English (Orconera, Tharsis and above all the Río Tinto mines, which were bought in 1873 for 93 million pesetas and declared in 1921 a capital of 337 million). Foreign companies naturally concentrated on the export of raw materials—an economical proposition given the cheap labour force. Thus Spain hardly benefited from her own resources.

Plant (machinery, transport, power) had the same problems. Spain in a capitalist Europe was caught in the vicious circle of all poor and underdeveloped countries. To make money, you need plant; to get plant, you need money. An excellent report of the Surveyors of Roads and Bridges put this clearly in 1840 *à propos* of the first railway concessions. National prosperity could hardly be expected to create the railways; railways had to be created to promote national prosperity. This is the proper stand to take in favour of getting plant first in the economic circuit, but it was too advanced a stand. Concessions went abroad (above all to the Pereires). The only thing the government did was to commit a geographical howler by creating a radiating network around Madrid, later ruined by the construction of bad "secondary systems". Spain still suffers from these initial errors.

The birth of heavy industry and the second phase in plant acquisition demonstrated, between 1910 and 1920, the existence of similar laws. In search of rapid returns, motor transport ran in competition to, rather than in co-operation with, the railways; hydroelectric companies hastily constructed stations in the Pyrenees, first in competition and then together as a trust under the patronage of the Barcelona Traction, Power and Light Company (La Canadiense). Other trusts sprang up (Pirelli, Siemens, I.G. Farben); Suria potash was shared out between several agencies. So that Spain took the burden of a productive system, not nationally controlled; and this system, in yielding to the pressures already built up, further emphasised the contrast between the large rural areas and the few specialised industrial ones.

(b) *Light industry*

This, however, between 1830 and 1890, was able to realise with modest national capital the developments initiated in the eighteenth century. In Catalonia a textile industry emerged, not in large-scale units, but geographically grouped around the Barcelona communication network—2 million cotton spindles, 50,000 looms; a woollen industry located in two towns (Tarrassa, Sabadell); an excellent hosiery trade; leather, paper, cork, printing, light machinery works. Barcelona grew from 88,000 inhabitants in 1818 to 190,000 in 1860, and 510,000 in 1897. The firms were average-sized, based on family capital, needing only modest financial backing. But as the capital was national and this was more or less the only consumer industry in Spain, the Catalans considered themselves "the workers of the nation". Because they could not compete with England, and since the colonial markets were from that time on restricted, they elaborated protectionism into a doctrine which was almost a mystique. Both Güell Ferrer and Bosch Labrús showed the same doctrinaire spirit as List, the German proponent of the Zollverein. Their mouthpiece was the "Fomento del Trabajo Nacional". They organised the press, meetings and parliamentary pressure groups; they denounced Madrid policy and the burden of the rest of poverty-stricken Spain; they wanted to direct the nation's economy. But liberal anglophiles and agrarian conservatives in turn denounced the industrial egoism of Catalonia. Thus the process of industrialisation became involved with important political issues: foreign affairs, regionalism and social questions.

4. POLITICAL PROBLEMS
ISSUING FROM SPANISH ECONOMIC DEVELOPMENT

(a) *Foreign and colonial affairs*

Politically weak, Spain was naturally treated as a sphere of influence by foreign powers. Intervention in 1823, policies *vis-à-vis* carlism, the "Spanish marriages", the intrigues around Espartero and Narváez, all these are episodes in Anglo-French rivalry over Spain. The role of England in the independence of the colonies, in the control of the mines, the struggle of Cobden against textile tariffs, the moves of Mendizábal, Espartero and the free-traders all demand investigation. Spain may have avoided the satellite position accepted by Portugal, but her riches and her geographical position never ceased to attract schemers from abroad.

On the other hand, there was never any question of Spain reasserting herself in the colonial sphere. After the loss of the Empire, the first attempt of this sort took place in Morocco in 1859; but this did not lead to any firm penetration. And when the Algeciras agreement approved a Spanish Morocco for reasons of equilibrium, the attempts at occupation created grave internal repercussions (1909). In 1898 Cuba, Puerto Rico, Guam and the Philippines were lost. This impotence did not leave Spain unmoved. Costa advised a real "African policy" (i.e. one not limited to military ends), but the defeat of 1898 crystallised a political opposition which had been formulated by the intelligentsia. This defeat brought its economic consequences. It removed from industry its last foreign markets, thus reinforcing protectionism. The Catalans, with their contempt for

74   SPAIN: A BRIEF HISTORY

Madrid and for the low level of life in the rural areas redoubled
their claims to lead the nation. It was the time of Prat de la Riba's
exaltation of the "imperialism of the producers" in *La Nacionalitat
catalana*, itself a disquieting title. In 1900, as in 1640 and 1700,
political weakness at the centre led to revolt in the more dynamic
areas of the Peninsula.

(b) *The regionalist problem*

It is curious to see how the "nationalist" movements had such
damaging effect on a structure as old and venerable as united Spain.
But we know that the Hapsburg monarchy did not play the same
role in unification as the French kings, nor the Cadiz Cortes the
same role as the French Revolution. In the nineteenth century both
carlism on the right and federalism on the left illustrate the centrifugal tendency. But there is more to it than that: at the end of the
century, the different regions acquired a group consciousness to such
a degree that they called themselves "nations".

"Basque nationalism" is above all a twentieth-century development, although it was born in the nineteenth under its apostle Sabino
Arana. It appeared first in Bilbao, which means that it may be defined not so much as a heritage of the old *forismo* than the reaction
of an economically advanced region against political direction from
a backward capital.

"Catalanism" is earlier in appearance, and in the challenge it
posed, responds even better to such a definition. Nevertheless, it
started as a *felibrige* movement. The Catalan language rediscovered
its literary nobility between 1833 and 1850 with Aribau's *Oda a la
Pàtria*, the poems of Rubió i Ors, and the *Jocs Florals*. The historical
works of the Bofarulls, Milá Fontanals, and Balaguer brought the
Catalan past back into fashion. Great poets, Verdaguer and later
Maragall, appeared. The real question is how did this intellectual
movement, of no greater literary value than that of Mistral, acquire
a theatre, a press, institutions and finally leave its mark on a whole
people instead of remaining confined to the work of coteries and
ephemeral publications?

Without doubt "land, race and tongue" can define Catalonia. Nevertheless the pressure of these factors is not continuous—they had been almost forgotten between 1750 and 1830. Moreover, Cerdagne and Roussillon failed to provide any political platform, and the recovery of the language (above all the work of Pompeu Fabra between 1910 and 1925) followed rather than preceded political enthusiasm for independence. This means that the true issue does not lie with these "differentiating factors" (geography, ethnics, language, law, psychology, history) but with other reasons which had inspired a given region at a given time to bring these factors forward once again. These may be seen in two ways—on one hand the impotence of the Spanish State; on the other the growing difference between the social structure of the Catalan area and that of the majority of the nation.

Impotence of the State? Let us remember that after the times of Charles III the State had not been actively successful; it had made no considered effort to spread the myth of community—and in particular no large-scale educational effort.

Difference in structure? In Catalonia there existed a dynamic bourgeoisie, and all sorts of well-off middle class social levels, intent on hard work, thrift and private enterprise, attracted by protectionism, political liberty and the development of purchasing power. In Spain the old way of life predominated: the peasant worked to live and not to sell; the landowner neither built up capital nor invested; the *hidalgo*, to avoid the loss of social status, sought refuge in the army or the church; the Madrid bourgeoisie sought it in politics or administration; conservatives condemned political liberty and liberals protectionism—two structures, two psychologies which were to inflame each other by their polemics.

These polemics arose in every discussion of finance or taxes. Meetings, articles, parliamentary debates, official reports rocked Catalonia, fused the regional pride of the intellectuals with the arguments of the economists and popular discontent. This agitation almost always carried the day and at the same time the idea of regional solidarity gathered force. In the non-industrial areas a general attack was launched on the Catalan commercial traveller as the type who exploited others and put up the cost of living, accompanied by all the sarcasm that pre-capitalist psychology reserves for the businessman. So two images grew up—the Castilian seeing only the abrupt, money-grubbing, petty-minded Catalan; the Catalan on the other hand the proud and lazy Castilian.

One can see here a double inferiority complex—in the Catalan case, a political one; in the Castilian case, an economic one—leading to unbridgable mistrust, in which language was the rallying point and history an arsenal of arguments.

This explains the evolution of Catalanism itself. From a regionalist movement with an intellectual basis it passed to an independence movement (1892, "Bases de Manresa") and after 1898, to a nationalist movement. In 1906 the "Solidaritat Catalana" party got an electoral majority over all other parties. At the same time another significant point was reached. Ever since the first Catalan political party, the "Lliga Regionalista" was able to unite the mainly moderate elements (well-off scholars, energetic industrialists, Catholic peasants and small shopkeepers), Madrid hoped to rely on the demagogue Lerroux, idol of the Barcelona masses, to counterbalance it. But Lerroux was disqualified in 1909 by his inglorious role after the "Semana Trágica". From then on Catalanism became the focus for a democratic and *petit bourgeois* type of opposition—a "left wing" Catalanism which brought together small landowners, "rabassaires", salaried workers, civil servants and middle class intellectuals. A regionalist *bloc* had established itself against Madrid.

(c) *Social movements and workers' organisations*

In the nineteenth century the percentage of industrial population was never high—three regional nuclei (Catalonia, Asturias, the Basque provinces), four or five towns (Madrid, Seville, Valencia, Málaga, Saragossa), isolated mining areas (Peñarroya, Río Tinto, la Unión)—this was a rickety basis for a working-class movement of the English or German type. Nevertheless, from the nineteenth century onwards, the working class in Spain has played a significant

role. In the twentieth, one may speak of "anarchist" Spain, "syndi-
calist" Spain, "marxist" Spain—general terms of abuse, but significant ones, for the Spanish proletariat has had a more important
historical role than its small numbers would lead one to expect.
Does it not recall Lenin's analysis of Russia? In a country predomi-
nantly agricultural where the agrarian situation was serious, where
an out-of-date aristocracy was crumbling away in one political
disaster after another, where the middle classes had little social
weight, might not a few proletarian nuclei, over-exploited by
capital frequently foreign, be sufficient to give a firm direction to
working-class movements? Precisely because of this Lenin saw
Spain as the appointed country for a second revolution, and the
parallel Spain/Russia was on everybody's lips between 1917 and
1923, either to announce or denounce the imminence of social
collapse. Furthermore, the Spanish revolutionary·movement was
backed by local tradition.

In Catalonia, from 1830 to 1860 the trend towards workers'
associations was already marked ("Sociedad de Tejedores", "Las
tres clases de vapor", "Unión manufacturera") as were outbursts of
violence (machine-breaking in 1835, general strike in 1855) and
public disturbances after political incidents (1835, 1840, 1854). This
was probably more persistent than the present inadequate research
reveals, since the emergence of workers' organisations in 1868
cannot be explained without a previous period of incubation.

In 1868, Fanelli, Bakunin's disciple, arrived in Spain. He founded
sections of the "International Workers' Association" and, in greater
secrecy, units of the Bakunin "Alliance of Social Democracy". Their
success was phenomenal—in a few months the "Federation", an
organ of the International, had more than 100,000 adherents in two
main centres, Catalonia and Andalusia. Spain became at that moment
with France of the Commune a major field of experiment for the
international revolutionary movement. From London Marx and
Engels took issue with the bakuninists in Switzerland in an obstinate
struggle over Spain. James Guillaume has left a record of it. Engels
has also left in a well-known pamphlet his criticism of the canton-
alist movement after its failure, a basic text of the marxists' attack on

the anarchists. However, despite a fruitful mission by Lafargue, bakuninism won through in the end. The division, however, persisted after the reconstitution of workers' organisations following the 1874–76 repression.

The "Partido Socialista Obrera" was born at that moment in Madrid and developed a trade union organisation in 1888, the "Unión General de Trabajadores" (UGT). It was successful in areas of large-scale industrial concentration (Asturian mines, Basque metallurgy), among educated workers in Madrid, symbolised by the party's founder, the typographer Pablo Iglesias, an unoriginal but noble figure who maintained Spanish socialism for a long time in the tradition of Lafargue and Guesde. Later this tradition was gradually forgotten under the influence of pure politicians (Indalecio Prieto) or of university lawyers (Besteiro, Jiménez Asúa, Fernando de los Ríos) and replaced by parliamentary politics and reform through legislation. The revolutionary spirit of the Spaniards, however, was moving to another channel.

In 1881, in effect, fifty militants from Barcelona had also founded a workers' "federation", anarchist in inspiration. In two years (with congresses in Seville and Valencia) it had attracted 50,000 supporters; as usual, 30,000 came from Andalusia, 13,000 from Catalonia. Repression and internal divisions made its existence difficult. Anarchism, however, between 1890 and 1910 had gone through a heroic period —"direct action" by assassination, strikes in 1890 and 1902, the Montjuich affair and the "Semana Trágica". A more organised phase dated from 1911 with the foundation of an anarcho-syndicalist union. This "Confederación Nacional del Trabajo" or CNT dominated the working-class movement in Spain until the Civil War.

More important than the anarchism of the nineties (an international phenomenon) was the continued persistence of the movement into contemporary times. It is too easy to explain this away as a question of temperament. Why should the Spain of Cisneros and the "Tribunal de las Aguas", or Catalonia with its characteristic "prudence" and its co-operatives be "peculiarly" suited to individualistic forms of social revolution? It would be more to the point (and

less simple) to analyse Spanish anarchism in relation to the structure and the historical past of the areas from which it arose, for
example:

(i) Links of the workers' movement with the agrarian problem;
anarchist journals with the titles *Tierra, Tierra y libertad*; Andalusian
peasant revolts which haunt the Spaniards' nightmare of revolution.

(ii) The small unit structure of Catalan industry: the gap between
employer and employee was narrow here and the struggle retained
a personal note.

(iii) The wretchedness of city life: on top of the workers' distress,
there was the distress of the immigrant, unemployment, casual
labour, sordid living conditions (the *distrito quinto* in Barcelona). The
phenomenon of the "factory" itself does not seem to bulk so large,
but the urban masses were highly sensitive, continuously seething,
and ripe for provocation.

(iv) The relations between the working-class movement and
politics. Nineteenth-century politics were a constant disappointment, which explains the worker's "political apathy"; but at the
same time, in the face of constant police tyranny, he acquired a
passion for freedom and a hatred of the State. Liberalism had for
him a secret attraction, and this accounts for the pendulum movement in Spanish elections; after a spell of the "left", disappointed
anarchists call for abstention, *no votad*; this abstention brings a
favourable poll for the "right"; after a period of "right" rule, the
rebellious worker renounces abstention, but he has no candidate to
vote for; the "left" gets in but the worker is not represented.

(v) The revolutionary tradition. Díaz del Moral has demonstrated the important part played by *tradition* in the Andalusian
revolts. Barcelona anarchism also had its past, its memories and its
martyrs; and the sentimental echoes of such a past set up a barrier
for a long time against socialism and communism.

(vi) Finally, the pattern of thought. When Anselmo Lorenzo, the
patriarch of Spanish anarchism, visited Marx in London in 1870 he
reacted like a frightened, awe-struck, self-taught man. From then on
he preferred to give his sympathy to the instinctive passions of the

working-class movement, to sentimental and impassioned doctrines rather than to the "bourgeois science" of marxism. Lorenzo organised with the help of Francisco Ferrer a veritable educational organisation, all the more influential because the official primary schools did nothing for the majority of illiterate youth. The "Escuela Moderna", cheap pamphlets and the "Ateneos Populares" left their mark on whole generations. This educational system was held to be more all-embracing (more "encyclopaedic") than the marxist equivalent, but it left the militant revolutionaries less prepared to tackle the real problems. Anarchism absorbed deeply rooted Spanish traits—personal loyalty, admiration for the individual gesture and above all the desire for liberation, more instinctive than rational, from the ancestral pressures of religion. In this respect, it was only another instance of a larger problem which had unceasingly troubled the entire century—the ideological struggle.

(d) *Ideological issues*

These arose, as in the eighteenth century, out of a double conflict. The desire for regeneration fought against the weight of tradition. At the same time the desire for regeneration was opposed by the nation's pride in its own particular achievements.

The first half of the century contributed little to the conflict. The romantic movement was a literary one and the liberal movement a mere copy, much more so than in the eighteenth century. Spain of the *ancien régime* was a mere vestige of its former self, and by 1840 it was a hollow shell. This was just sufficient to ensure the persistence of touching medieval customs in remote places, but not enough to protect the faith in urban centres and other areas of contact. In mid-century a Catalan priest, Balmes, and a converted liberal, Donoso Cortés, made a strong appeal for the revival of tradition, but they were on the defensive, and their influence was not immediately apparent. The inattentive mass of Spanish clergy maintained its claim to be the exclusive leader of the nation, without any evidence of cultural improvement on its part. Religious solidarity was confused with the maintenance of religious practices, and even today the foreigner in Spain will be surprised both by the force of the religious subconscious and the average man's ignorance of the basic elements of Roman Catholicism. In attacks on religion, or in its defence, the intellectual element was negligible, which explains the impassioned nature of the dispute, evidence in itself of the failure of popular education—school and catechism were all one. This failure is difficult to refute. Although the Spanish Church may have dreamed in the twentieth century of leading a new Counter Reformation, there was no parallel in the nineteenth to Cisneros' pre-Reformation, or to the educating force of the sixteenth-century clergy. Contemporary spiritual movements in Spain, even in their mystical and traditional aspects, occurred *outside* or *in opposition to* the Church—they were "intellectual" movements.

Between 1860 and 1880 one can discern three facets. First, a crop of novels of varying worth, interesting in their orientation. Pereda defends the old Spain, not without irony. Valera, Palacio Valdés, Pardo Bazán criticise it, but not without compassion. Leaving aside their differences, all these writers had one preoccupation—to isolate and define "national" and "Spanish" elements. They disclose a people in the grip of a moral dilemma, self-questioning but devoted to their own idiosyncracies.

Another intellectual current, apparently quite different in its origins, was the "Krausista" movement, imported from German universities in the forties by a young man on a government scholarship, Julián Sanz del Río, whose influence, between 1855 and 1865, brought about a small-scale "Reformation". It was less a question of ideas than of an attitude to life, but from it emerged a lay spiritualism with rigid principles and a faith in education which fired the men of the First Republic. The expansion of its field of action came much later. If one also bears in mind that in this later period, 1865–75, the two main currents of Spanish revolutionary thought emerged out of the Marx–Bakunin quarrel, it is highly likely that the sources from which present-day Spain draws its inspiration are to be found in that decade, rather than in the "generación del 98", to which they are generally ascribed. This usual hypothesis is acceptable only as long as one defines this generation in the widest possible sense so as to include all manner of reaction to the new "obsession with decadence" which the defeat of 1898 rendered intolerable.

After 1880 "Krausismo", with Francisco Giner de los Ríos, penetrated into education. A quasi-university, the "Institución Libre de Enseñanza", undertook a revision of teaching methods and research which blossomed in 1912 into the official "Junta para Ampliación de Estudios", with secondary schools, centres for scientific study and scholarships for study abroad. The educational pattern was new—projects, excursions, co-education, a passion for nature study and folk-lore, and a preference for biology and sociology. Thanks to the "Institución", Spain not only equalled but often surpassed her neighbours in higher education. But one reservation must be made; this did not touch the "Old Spain", faithful to its religious education, nor the lower classes who were still deprived—around 1900 more than half of the population could not read. So the "Krausista" intelligentsia remained an artificial phenomenon, isolated and of limited impact. When they later achieved power, these characteristics may be seen to have some relation with their lack of experience and authority.

One may also associate with the "Institución" those historians and sociologists of the years 1890–1900, still ill-equipped, but excellent pioneers, whose work recalls the eighteenth century in its pursuit of universality and sympathy for the national past. Such a one was Joaquín Costa who sought like an anguished soul for Spanish traits in common law, folk-lore, rural economy, and communal irrigation practices. Hinojosa and Altamira, with more science, laid the foundations for a social and psychological study of their country. After 1898 Costa threw himself into active politics, massed the Aragonese peasantry against the tax-collector, calling himself first a republican and later a revolutionary. He invented all sorts of proposals for the future, like a twentieth-century *arbitrista*. At the time he acquired a reputation but his glory passed away quickly beside that of more brilliant writers. From then on the "Generation of 1898" took an exclusively literary turn.

Just as Quevedo condemned *arbitrismo* in the name of a proud despair, so, around 1898, there were many who, united in their contempt for positive action, wrote lyrical commentaries on their disillusion with Spain. They formed no school—their temperaments were quite different—but their writings revolved around the same pride and the same bitterness. Baroja trampled on tradition but remained deaf to voices from outside. Antonio Machado, the young teacher in Soria, centred his poetic meditations on the landscape of Old Castile, but denounced "la sangre de Caín", the "estómago vacío y alma huera" of the Spaniard. Ganivet died in despair far from his country, after having written his *Idearium* to prove that Spain and Europe have nothing in common. Unamuno claimed first place for his country in that rebellion against technology and faith in progress which was springing up everywhere around the same period. He delighted in turning well-known formulae upside down, and proposed the Hispanisation of Europe with Don Quixote as the symbol. Unamuno was the greatest genius with words that Spain had known for centuries, but his word-juggling and paradoxes sowed contradiction and doubt in the minds of later generations.

The first contradiction is that the scientific spirit inherited from Giner, which inspired many brilliant schools of philology, history, biology, or figures like Menéndez Pidal, Sánchez Albornoz or Marañón, was married to a perilous fascination for literary brilliance and philosophical snobbery derived from Ortega y Gasset and Eugenio d'Ors.

The second contradiction is that Spanish writers following on those of '98 became *engagé* to the point of considering themselves, after the 1931 crisis, to be the destined moral directors of the New Spain. The fact is that they could not convince either the Old Spain, who maligned them, or the proletariat whom they themselves did not know. When they came face to face in politics with the violence of physical struggle they withdrew, some noisily, others in silence, and not without some contempt for those who still remained *engagé*, thus provoking in present-day Spain a further drama of spiritual schism and doubt.

The last contradiction is that the '98 writers wanted to criticise the Spanish character and at the same time elaborate and ennoble the myth around it. Some of their disciples only retained the ability to criticise—they were the disillusioned. Others retained only the arrogance—and they were to turn the simplified theses of Ganivet and Unamuno into the racial theories of the nazis and the Imperial dreams of the fascists. Maeztú might have wanted it thus—but Azorín accepted it implicitly. Unamuno, however, was to have his moment of anguish on his death-bed.

Nevertheless, as always in Spain, there was to emerge a synthesis between the spirit of tradition and the refusal to conform. But for that one needed the genius of Federico García Lorca, Miguel Hernández or Pablo Picasso, and a great popular surge—that of 1936.

CHAPTER 5

THE CONTEMPORARY CRISIS

I. THE CRISIS OF THE MONARCHY (1917-31)

1. FIRST PHASE (1917–23). THE TIME OF THE TROUBLES

(a) *The crisis of 1917*

The economic euphoria due to the war subsided in 1917. The high cost of living, the news of the Russian revolution, disreputable speculation, clashes between *aliadófilos* and *germanófilos* inflamed and divided opinions.

In May *military unrest* gave shape to the agitation. Infantry officers formed *juntas* against favouritism. First condemned, and later pardoned, they claimed to offer an example "to all those who felt the need for good government". Non-commissioned officers and post-office workers also formed *juntas* and this led to *political unrest*. Regionalists, reformers, radicals and socialists called for a meeting of the Cortes, where the government's majority was not assured. An illegal group of eighty opposition members met in Barcelona and demanded the recall of the Constituent Assembly. They were dispersed—"a simple matter for the police", said the government: a well-used phrase which matched ill the gravity of the crisis! At the end of July, *social unrest* replaced political agitation. There were strikes in Valencia, Bilbao and Santiago; *juntas* were formed even amongst the security police. On 13 August there was a general strike; on 15 August machine-guns fired and killed at Cuatro Caminos (Madrid); there were pitched battles in Catalonia and the mining north. But the government carried the day. The socialist leaders (Saborit, Anguiano, Besteiro, Caballero) were arrested; other politicians (Lerroux, Macià) managed to escape. Maura and General

Primo de Rivera protested publicly against government weakness. Although the régime lasted for another five years, it was in the midst of rising confusion.

(b) The Time of the Troubles (1917–23)

The "ministerial dance" led to political chaos: in six years, thirteen serious crises, thirty less serious ones. The "great cabinet" of Maura, Romanones and Cambó collapsed. Maura became more intransigent to Catalan demands and Cambó returned to the opposition with the famous speech, "Monarchy? Republic? Catalonia!": the regional issue became acute once more.

Social confusion became worse. The high cost of living disturbed the white-collar workers. In 1919 an industrial crisis occurred, but it was rural Spain that rose first. 1918–21 is called in Andalusia "the Bolshevik triennium"; passionately intent on breaking up the large estates, the peasants wrote on the walls of the *cortijos* "Viva Lenin" although this does not imply any communist indoctrination on the part of the leaders. When the socialist party divided in 1921, only the Basque provinces seemed attracted to communism. The great focus of attraction was still the non-political and quasi-anarchist trade unionism.

The CNT Congress in Sabadell (1919) represented 300,000 supporters. The *Canadiense* (the electrical company in Catalonia) strike marked the apogee of the trade union movement. Two leaders stand out, Salvador Seguí ("el noi del sucre") and Angel Pestaña. The government opened discussion with them and accepted the "eight-hour day". But an aggressive management imposed a lock-out. This unleashed a campaign of terror which flamed through Catalonia, Saragossa and Bilbao. In June, in Barcelona, the two symbols of repression were General Martínez Anido and the police chief Arlegui. They matched *pistolero* with *pistolero* and employer-dominated unions (*sindicatos libres*) with CNT-dominated ones (*sindicatos únicos*). They mobilised the reserve police force of the *somaten*, and used the *ley de fugas* in order to shoot escaping prisoners. Salvador Seguí was murdered, then his counsel. Public opinion became indignant, and Martínez Anido was relieved in October 1922. But faced with an increased number of assassinations the Catalan pressure groups (commercial and industrial leaders) declared their support for the Captain General of the area, Primo de Rivera. This was the sign for a regrouping of the "partisans of order".

At the same time the Moroccan problem was also in need of a solution. Morocco had always been considered quite openly by the Spaniards as a field for the army's personal ambitions and the financial interests of politicians. For this reason they made sacrifices in this area with the worst of grace.

On 21 July 1921, General Silvestre had been murdered with his headquarter staff in an ambush at Annual. The Riff had revolted during the disorderly retreat, leaving 14,000 dead or captured. From 1921 to 1923 General Berenguer pleaded incessantly for money and reinforcements to carry out a painful reconquest. The King (accused of secretly influencing the military command), his ministers and the "Juntas" passed responsibility from one to another. Politicians from all sides protested—Maura, Cambó, the socialist Prieto and General Primo de Rivera himself, who made an unexpected speech to the Senate in favour of abandoning Morocco. Removed from Castile to Catalonia, and profiting by the social unrest there, he prepared for the role he was to take up later.

On 13 September 1923, assured of the support of the upper middle classes and the garrisons, he proclaimed himself head of a "Directorate" to which the King assented. None came to the defence of a discredited parliamentary regime, and this tended later to fortify the mistaken belief in the inevitable apathy of the Spanish people faced with a pronunciamiento.

2. SECOND PHASE (1923–30). DICTATORSHIP

The political history of the dictatorship is quickly told. The "military Directorate" became a civil one at the end of 1925 and in 1927 a Consultative Assembly, a constitution was planned in 1929— but none of this changed its substance or its methods. Did it in fact, resolve any of the great national problems facing it?

Only the Moroccan question. The French alliance was maintained and after 1925 no more was heard of the Riff. On the other hand, the Moroccan army (the legion or the *tercio*—regular native troops) was to become a powerful independent instrument in the hands of its generals.

Important *economic projects* had been announced by two men—the Count of Guadalhorce and Calvo Sotelo. They were accused of increasing the Public Debt—18,000 million pesetas of floating debt from 1926, and a 1000 million budget deficit in 1928. But the State went on financing major public works. One at least was far-reaching —the "Confederaciones Sindicales Hidrográficas". Costa's dream seemed to be taking shape. The State required agricultural and industrial enterprises in each river basin to combine in order to finance, with State aid, an organised scheme of water distribution, irrigation and electrification. One particular association made great strides in the Ebro valley because a famous engineer Lorenzo Pardo took the opportunity to bring to fruition certain long-hoped-for plans—a dam in the upper reaches of the Ebro, reservoirs on the slopes of the Pyrenees, an extension of the Catalano-Aragonese canal, in all a most significant set of hydrological studies. Unfortunately his work suffered from inaccurate budgeting and scheming contractors. It was also an isolated achievement, which none of the other "Confederaciones" could match. The industrialists were cautious and the farmers had little capital, so the State carried the major burden. The plans stayed on paper and the "Confederaciones" were covered with the same discredit as the dictatorship itself, which, through its 1929 Exhibition and its network of motor roads, had been charged with megalomania.

The more theoretical plans (economic nationalism, state-directed economy) had produced even fewer successes. The decreed percentage of national investment and native technical employment in business enterprises was not observed. The telephone monopoly went to the Americans; the incentives given to Andalusian ports and encouragement for the geographical dispersal of industry did not modify the existing structure, and annoyed both Basques and Catalans. Finally the offers of government posts in the Department

of Economic Affairs to interested parties and army officers, the sub-
sidising of failing railway and commercial companies created so
much scandal that it was forbidden to circulate rumours. The dictatorship was immersed in the very situation it had intended to
combat. Nevertheless, it was able to profit from the remarkable
world-wide prosperity and attributed to itself some of the credit for
it. That in itself brought several disadvantages. Big business, with
the wind behind it, saw only the black side of state intervention. It
was a costly régime, and it was discarded.

The *social programme* had announced, as in Italy, the "suppression
of the class struggle": compulsory arbitration boards were set up;
the social reformers Caballero and Prieto were invited to collabor-
ate; night work by women was made subject to legislation. But the
workers complained that wages were not following the remarkable
upward trend of management prosperity, and that strikes had been
made illegal. More serious was the neglect of the agrarian problem:
4000 were resettled on 20,000 hectares with a financial allotment of
2 million pesetas, according to the most favourable figures: others
made it out to be ten times less. In any case these figures do not
measure up to the necessary reforms. In 1930 it was clear that the
social struggle still remained acute.

The *regional problem* was tackled, not on a grand scale but with a
remarkable meanness of vision. The 1912 "Mancomunitat" of
Catalonia and its work were destroyed, and agreement with the
Basque and Catalan leading classes was soon lost. But as their
regional patriotism had become suspect, support for local national
feeling came henceforward from the democratic opposition, with
the result that the moral unity of Spain was increasingly threatened.

The *political failure* was in the end obvious to all. The fascist
imitation had been superficial—no mass party, no mystique of
youth. The "Unión Patriótica" and the civilian militia had simply
carried on the old *cacique* system. Primo, nevertheless, kept up for a
long time the façade of optimism, making use of either his geniality
or brusque appeals to the masculine virtues. He exiled Unamuno,
despatched the student leaders to Cuenca, and created disaffection in
the artillery: Macià had tried a romantic but moving *coup* in 1926

at Prats de Molló: in 1929 an attempted pronunciamiento took place in Ciudad Real: Sánchez Guerra, the champion of constitutional legality, disembarked at Valencia to overthrow the régime, failed but was acquitted. The peseta fell. Neither financiers nor foreigners had any further confidence in the dictatorship. The military leaders, on being consulted, blew cold and Primo de Rivera retired on 30 January 1930, dying shortly afterwards in Paris. It is well known that one of his sons, José Antonio, was to profit from these lessons in the formation of a new fascist movement.

3. THIRD PHASE (1930–31). THE COLLAPSE OF THE MONARCHY

The semi-dictatorship, headed by General Berenguer, could only be transitional. The old parties came to life again under García Prieto, Romanones, Sánchez Guerra, Melquiades Alvarez and Cambó. The anti-monarchists signed the "Agreement of San Sebastián" in favour of the establishment of a Republic. The signatories were Miguel Maura, Alcalá Zamora (moderates); Lerroux, Martínez Barrio (radicals) and younger party leaders like Azaña, Quiroga, A. de Albornoz, M. Domingo; also republican Catalanists like Nicolau d'Olwer and the socialists (Caballero, Prieto, de los Ríos.) This was a political committee, and it had a delicate problem of exploring relations with the trade-unions whose support was sought, but whose armed strength was feared. November 1930 was a month of profound social unrest.

Nevertheless the political events were more striking: the return of Unamuno and Macià, the game of hide-and-seek played by Franco's Air Force brother with the police, student demonstrations. The long-awaited conclusion came at last on 12 December: the Jaca garrison proclaimed the Republic and marched on Huesca. Was this a misunderstanding or difference of opinion, for it had anticipated the Committee's timetable? At Ayerbe it met with military resistance. The two leaders, Captains Galán and García Hernández, were shot, and the Republic acquired its first martyrs. On 15 December the Air Force tried in vain to launch the movement once again. The Republican Committee was then put in prison.

However, this was merely a postponement. "La realeza debe ceder a la realidad", said Sánchez Guerra. Political parties refused to take part in elections under a semi-dictatorship. Berenguer yielded to the last and mainly monarchist Cabinet—Cierva, García Prieto, Romanones and Ventosa—which organised a superficially harmless municipal poll. Half of the rural municipalities elected unopposed *caciques*; but on 12 April the urban municipal elections outstripped all expectations—the Left was triumphant everywhere. On 14 April Eibar, Barcelona, San Sebastián proclaimed the Republic; in Madrid, Romanones had discussions with Alcalá Zamora. Sanjurjo, head of the Civil Guard, refused to guarantee the regime any further, and the King had to resign himself to abdication. It was almost a day of apotheosis. Old republicans and intellectuals, faced with this blood- less revolution, thought that Spain had reached the climax of politi- cal maturity. The working classes, ever deeply affected by the mention of liberty, hoped for great things, and one day José Antonio Primo de Rivera himself was to recognise that 14 April had a special place in the history of Spain. The idea "that something had to be changed" seemed to have been accepted by every Spaniard. But what? The Republic would have to provide the answer.

II. THE REPUBLIC (1931-36)

The Dictatorship had ruled, but it had made no changes: the Republic wanted to make changes, but had difficulty in ruling. At least it did attempt to tackle, in its first years, all the major problems. The Constituent Cortes, elected in May 1931, had produced a very compact republican and socialist majority and the intention to re- form seemed beyond question.

1. 1931–33. TWO YEARS OF REFORM ("EL BIENIO REFORMADOR")

For the majority of the members of the Cortes, intellectuals, lawyers and old politicians, the constitutional, educational, ecclesi- astical and military issues which had dominated the nineteenth century were paramount.

(a) *The political issues*

The *Constitution* was modelled on that of Weimar, the most democratic in all Europe. Spain was proclaimed "the Workers' Republic", not without causing some amusement. Parliamentarianism unalloyed carried the day—a single chamber, complete ministerial responsibility, universal suffrage including women and soldiers. Nevertheless, the idea of the "moderating power" played a considerable part. The president of the Republic could dissolve the Chamber twice, as long as he subsequently justified his decision (the first President, Alcalá Zamora, was to lend considerable significance to this role of the political moderator). A Tribunal of Constitutional Guarantees was to pronounce on all constitutional irregularities. "Statutes" of autonomy could be requested, but the word "federal" did not appear anywhere. Finally the country renounced war and became a member of the League of Nations.

The founders of the Republic, professors, intellectuals from the "Ateneo" and the "Agrupación al servicio de la República" also concerned themselves with *education and scholarship*. The "Institución Libre" became a model for the universities and the "Institutos" of secondary education. The primary schools presented greater problems. To build up a lay educational structure after the French manner would have meant 27,000 new schools; but the estimates voted were only sufficient for seven or eight thousand—there was also a shortage of teachers. Finally any quarrel with the religious orders over their 600,000 pupils would raise, besides practical issues, the most delicate of psychological problems, that of religion.

The *religious question* was serious. It was a big jump from the church of the *ancien régime* to the lay system of the French. The liberal Catholics (who were represented in parliament) would have accepted a "separation" which left the Church free and removed nothing of its actual power. But the republicans saw a danger in this power. They applied special laws (similar to those in France) to the Jesuits, the Orders and religious teaching establishments. This was not a new departure, but it cut deeply. Azaña declared that "Spain had ceased to be Catholic", and the semi-anarchist extreme

Left, "the Wild Boars" (*Jabalíes*), paraded this popular anti-clerical-ism which saw the struggle for or against "los curas y frailes" at the centre of every political problem. A centuries'-old tradition was re-vived on 11 May 1931; convents were set ablaze by small groups while the crowds looked on with ironic indifference. Cemeteries were secularised and crucifixes removed from schools—a victory for one side, but for the other an "intolerable" attack on "freedom". Priests protested and were brought up in the courts. The bishops advised lawful opposition only, but it was opposition all the same. Such a clash was serious for the new régime, weighed down with other tasks.

The question of the *armed forces* also had to be solved. Many military men had remained convinced royalists, and in order to weaken this professional bias, Azaña offered retirement on full pay to those officers who wanted it. Ten thousand accepted, but they retained, in spite of their full salary, the bitterness of conspirators on half-pay. The Civil Guard was another prickly issue. It was feared for its power and hated by the people, but no-one would face the risk of dissolving it, and Azaña preferred in the end to match it with an élite Assault Guard.

The *regional issue* was eventually resolved—but not without mis-givings. Macià had proclaimed "the Catalan Republic" on 14 April, an act that went beyond the San Sebastián agreement. After dis-cussion the ancient name of "Generalitat" was resuscitated, and Catalonia voted almost unanimous approval of its Statute. The Cortes debate was a painful one but Azaña managed to get a decision after a soundly phrased address. This "Statute" allowed the area to have government, parliament, administration, law courts, a budget and its own culture. The Catalans were well prepared for the even-tuality, but delicate problems of public order (would there be a separate police force?) and the transfer of public services prolonged discussion. The Basques also elaborated their own "Statute" with enthusiasm. How many other areas would do the same? The Castilians talked ironically of presenting their own "Statute". The principle of national unity was becoming an excellent opposition platform.

(b) *Social problems*

Despite everything the social response to current hopes and fears quickly manifested itself. The lower classes looked forward to vital changes, while from April 1931 capital moved abroad.

Agrarian reform was the only basic reform explicitly promised. But there was no agreement yet on principles. "The land for those who work it", said the anarchists and the communists: "The land belongs to the State and its management to the peasant unions", said the socialists: "Private property", said the liberals: "Family property and substantial compensation for those expropriated", said the Catholics. The debate was lengthy and involved provisional guarantees: no expulsion of tenant farmers, no displacement of workers, distribution of Civil Lists monies to the unemployed.

The committee stage of the bill lasted up to May 1932, and the debate until 15 September. Then came the taking of the census. The bill was to apply only to the classic latifundist areas—Andalusia, Extremadura, La Mancha, Salamanca and Toledo. Expropriation was to take place above an "agricultural cum-social maximum" from about 10 hectares of well-irrigated land or 700 of poor pasture. Compensation, calculated by a capitalisation of 5–20 per cent according to means, was to be paid part in cash or part in 5 per cent bonds redeemable in fifty years. Nevertheless the peasant (wage-earner, tenant or small-holder) was only the beneficial owner and paid a small rent to the state. Incentives were given to encourage collective farming. An Institute of Agrarian Reform, provincial committees and local communities were to put reforms into practice. By 1933 they were to have settled 8600 families, expropriated 89,000 hectares and authorised the "temporary occupation" of more or less the same amount. This was very little, and was brought about in great measure by a political move—expropriation without compensation of the Spanish nobles involved in the attempted military *coup d'état* of August 1932. The pace of ordinary reform would have been much slower.

It is true that wages had gone up (by an average of 3 to 5 pesetas a day) and rents had gone down. But the associated fall in the price of land, the expectation of reform and peasant agitation led to the abandonment of a certain number of development schemes and a rise in unemployment. The socialists wanted to make use of the impatience of the peasant; in two years their "Federación de Trabajadores de la Tierra" could count on 392,000 members. It was thought they were looking for government support. But Andalusia stayed anarchist and the disturbances fell into the nineteenth-century pattern: squatting, tree-felling, poaching, sometimes arson. The daily brush with the Civil Guard took on an edge which alarmed public opinion. In Castilblanco the police were massacred, in Arnedo they fired on the town. The climax took place at Casas Viejas in Andalusia on 12 January 1933. This anarchist putsch was put down at a cost of twenty-one lives, of which twelve were arrested and officially executed. This time it was the work of the Assault Guards, and Azaña was held to be responsible. Thus the Casas Viejas incident became politically decisive, indicating that the over-cautious agrarian reform had not won the hearts of the peasants. For them, it was neither the night of 4 August nor Lenin's decree. And so in 1933 the rural proletariat turned away from the Republic and rejoined the urban proletariat in opposition.

The *working-class movement* at first smiled on the Republic. There were three socialists in power and the trade-union leaders in Barcelona (Pestaña, Peiró) had put their support behind Macià. Social legislation on the lines of the Geneva directives was quickly approved, and a policy of high wages was adopted. And this was in 1931–33, in the middle of a world slump! What they ought to have done, in order to avoid damaging production, was to have planned complete economic and monetary control. However, the Treasury was staffed by classic representatives of middle class capitalism with a liberal background, like the Catalan Carner. The paradox could not last, and when the socialist UGT wanted to limit wage demands, the anarcho-syndicalist CNT called them blacklegs.

Already in June 1931 Indalecio Prieto had thought it his duty to break a strike. Straight away came the reaction from the CNT. In May one of their congress meetings had approved the line of the moderates Pestaña and Peiró in Barcelona; in June criticism started;

by August the moderates were in a minority. After a sensational proclamation (known as the "Trentista" proclamation) these two were forced to abandon the leadership of the trade-union movement to the "Federación Anarquista Ibérica" (FAI) which took over the direction of the union newspaper *Solidaridad Obrera*. The Anarchist Durruti began to think he could make Barcelona and its workers once more into "the spiritual capital of the world".

In the end the government took savage measures. In July 1931 in Seville the first working-class victims fell; in September Governor Anguera de Sojo of Barcelona got the reputation of being another Martínez Anido; the "Law of the Defence of the Republic" worked out by Azaña and Anguera meant the suspension of the liberal guarantees in the Constitution. In January 1932 a rising took place in the Catalan highlands over textile wages (they wanted to push the scale from 12–30 pesetas to 25–40 a week); villages proclaimed "libertarian communism"; the army restored order and the leaders were deported to Villa Cisneros. Throughout the year working-class propaganda attacked the "Law of Defence" and supported the deportees. The FAI put its faith in a putsch and in January 1933 tried to combine a fresh general strike with peasant agitation. That was when the Casas Viejas drama occurred, and when Azaña became the target for a psychological offensive. The socialists were afraid to come to his support and, being isolated themselves, lost half their deputies in the November 1933 elections. Anarchist abstention, this time popularly approved, allowed the Right to gain an unexpected and disproportionate success.

So died the reformist, Jacobine Republic because it believed it could reform Spain by openly antagonising the strongest sector of the working-class movement, and by refusing immediate satisfaction to the peasant masses.

(c) *The opposition alliance and the failure of Azaña*

Opposition to Azaña and his parliamentary majority (itself in a critical state) increased. A centre opposition brought together doctrinaire liberals and conservative Republican supporters (two attitudes which in the main overlapped, although not always openly). The intellectuals mourned over a reality which was remote from their dreams and the press was full of the disappointment felt by Ortega and Unamuno. One man considered himself capable of governing at the centre—Lerroux, "republicano histórico", anti-socialist and erstwhile demagogue, who carried with him the more cautious sector of public opinion. However, army unrest and a growing sentimental *tradicionalismo* indicated that more brutal forms of opposition were on the way.

Right-wing opposition had given proof already of dissatisfaction with parliamentary procedure when, as a minority defeated on the religious issue, they had abandoned the Cortes. From 1931 there were plots amongst the generals. On 10 August 1932 Sanjurjo, former head of the Civil Guard (he had been relieved of command after the Arnedo incident), brought out the Seville garrison. This premature act failed to touch Madrid and strengthened Azaña for a while. The Right then returned to parliamentary opposition, but with internal divisions between "Agrarians", "Acción popular", "Renovación Española", monarchists, traditionalists, etc. Their slogans were negative, anti-Constitution, anti-secularisation, and the only bond was that of "España negra"; at the top, landed interests; at the bottom, tradition and religion. The clergy mobilised the feminine vote and opinion in the country. In the end emerged a partial coalition: the "Confederación Española de Derechos Autónomos" (CEDA) under an apparently impressive leader, Gil Robles.

At the same time there were emerging other new forms of opposition to which perhaps undue importance has been given, for in 1931–33 they were only starting to come to life as organisations. In 1931 *communism*, situated between socialism and anarcho-syndicalism, had shown little sign of activity. The Spanish communist party, a supporter of the Third International, had at that time barely 3000 members; its areas of recruitment were in the Asturias and the Basque provinces. Nevertheless, it had intervened in the July 1931 street fighting in Seville, and in Madrid there was a young enthusiastic minority. Moreover, this was for the party a period of doctrinal consolidation (the dogma of class warfare) and purges. It was the first to denounce the "bourgeois Republic" but its paper *Mundo Obrero*, irregular in appearance, small in format and often suppressed, could not compete with the socialist and anarchist press. There was no communist deputy in the first Cortes. Meanwhile, in Catalonia, the main working-class area, the "Federación Comunista Catalano-balear", or in its expanded form, the "Bloque Obrero y Campe-sino", was in open conflict with the International. Steering its way between catalanism and socialism, it had a number of good propa-gandists (Nin, Maurín, Arquer, Miravitlles) and an active press, but could not muster in 1931 more than 10,000 members. Thus com-munism (and even less "Moscow") did not play a significant role during the Republic except in the public imagination and in propa-ganda campaigns. But by its denunciation of reformist tendencies and apolitical groupings it soon attracted many disillusioned young anarchists eager to be indoctrinated and young socialists eager for action: only in 1936 were these potentials explored.

"*Fascism*" was the contemptuous name given by the Left to any Right-wing agitation. Gil Robles left himself open to this accusation by his visits to Germany, the organisation of rallies with symbolic slogans, and the salute of "Jefe, jefe" which he inaugurated. How-ever, more extremist elements later denounced him for his legalistic turn of mind and belief in parliamentarianism.

One of these elements came to life a month before 14 April 1931, with the first number of *La Conquista del Estado* by Ledesma and Giménez Caballero. The Hitlerian inspiration was beyond doubt, except that here the racist creed was replaced by the mystique of the Spanish imperial past. In Valladolid, in Onésimo Redondo's *Libertad*, the driving force was Castilian unity. These two tendencies converged in the "Juntas de Ofensiva Nacional Socialista" (JONS) in which "syndicalism" appeared as a "specifically" Spanish term. Their symbol (the yoke and arrows of Ferdinand and Isabel) was proposed by a student from Granada called Aparicio, and their programme appeared on 10 October 1931. It was anti-liberal, anti-marxist, anti-semitic, envisaging a State founded on *entidades protegidas*, the ideals of Spanish tradition, and the control of Gibraltar and Tangiers.

The "Falange" of José Antonio Primo de Rivera came shortly

afterwards. It was born out of small monarchist groups, persuaded by the analysis of the 1923 dictatorship made by the dictator's own son, who outlined his programme in the Comedia theatre, Madrid, on 29 October 1933: "Neither right nor left", neither capitalism nor socialism, but a revolution in our "way of life" and an appeal to the hero figure; Spain had turned down capitalism, reformism and liberalism; she alone was capable of leading "the twentieth-century revolution". The final appeal was lyrical and increased the prestige of the young leader; his recourse to violent action was well within tradition. The republicans, however, were hardly worried by a minority group equally distrusted by the traditionalist Right Wing, in which Gil Robles still appeared the more serious opponent.

Casas Viejas gave a pretext to the opposition coalition against Azaña. In April 1933 partial elections were unfavourable to him, as were the November elections to the Tribunal of Constitutional Guarantees. Alcalá Zamora then obliged him to resign. Lerroux failed to succeed him and in October 1933 Martínez Barrio was put in charge of a cabinet to dissolve the Constituent Cortes. Azaña, believing that the country was still with him, had passed an election law favourable to majority groups. The law, together with anarchist abstention, accentuated the adverse swing of opinion. Two hundred seats for the Right Wing, and 150 in the centre around Lerroux fore-shadowed a violent reaction against the Republic's first two years.

2. 1934–36. TWO YEARS OF REACTION ("EL BIENIO NEGRO")

(a) *Political, social and regional issues*

January to October 1934 brought a worsening of three issues, political, social and regional (Catalonia), which ended in violent conflict.

The *political situation* was full of difficulties. To avoid internal division the Right Wing did not support the Republic. The republican press declared that public opinion would not allow the régime to be handed over to its enemies. Lerroux governed therefore without the Right, but in their shadow. "We will take over when we want to", declared Gil Robles to a rally at the Escorial. The radical

Martínez Barrio disagreed with Lerroux, left him in April and in the summer split the party. The President of the Republic, disturbed by the Escorial rally and faithful to his role as a "moderator", personally refused to re-instal the rebel army leaders of the 1932 rising. In an atmosphere of disquiet Lerroux then handed over to Sampere, a second-rate radical.

Social disturbances had already begun with the elections. In December 1933 a "libertarian communist putsch" shook Aragon and Extremadura. The CNT, disorganised in principle, did not on that account fail to encourage strikes. Saragossa was paralysed in April and May by a general strike supported generously by workers in other cities. The situation was getting worse, with 600,000 out of work. The UGT opted for Largo Caballero as against Besteiro, that is, for revolutionary tactics. The events of February 1934 in France and Austria, and the communist "change of front" had left their mark. The slogan "unity" created the "Alianzas Obreras" and Prieto acknowledged that this impulse "came from the masses".

But amongst these 600,000 unemployed, 400,000 were peasants. The "Landworker's Federation" started agitating and in February arbitration boards (*jurados mixtos*) were reorganised to their disadvantage; land temporarily occupied was ordered to be vacated. In May the expropriation of landowners and decrees on rents and wages were annulled. The peasants attempted a "harvest strike". The government opposed the use of force, and declared there was "no trouble at all" when in fact there had been several deaths. The strike collapsed amidst great bitterness. The *regional issue* was linked to another agrarian conflict. Macià had died in late 1933 and the Catalan municipal elections confirmed a Left-wing majority. In contrast to Madrid the Generalitat had become a "bastion of the Republic", backing the claims of supporters of the controlling party ("Esquerra Catalana"), the land workers (CADCI) and the tenant farmers ("Rabassaires"). In April 1934 a "Ley de Cultivos" made it obligatory in certain cases for lands to be ceded to those tenants desirous of acquiring them. Landowners persuaded the regionalist "Lliga" to denounce the law to the Tribunal of Constitutional Guarantees as unconstitutional, and it was annulled. The Catalan

Parliament ratified it once more. The Basques for their part started to agitate and called illegal municipal elections.

At the end of the parliamentary holidays, Sampere's cabinet, accused of weakness in the face of so many incidents, was overthrown. Lerroux formed his own and took in three members of the CEDA. This was the test situation one had been waiting for.

Azaña called on "all possible means to defend the Republic"; Martínez Barrio and Sánchez Román refused "any collaboration" with the cabinet; even the moderate Miguel Maura denounced "this disfigured Republic". Would it only be a question of words? Madrid and Andalusia seemed a little tired of dissension, for the demonstrations were not widespread. But in two places two other revolutions broke out, the one quite distinct from the other.

(b) *October 1934. Revolution in Catalonia and Asturias*

In Catalonia the movement began at the top and failed nearly at once. Companys, Macià's successor in the Generalitat, backed on 5 October a general strike declared by the UGT and CADCI, dissident communists and Catalanist youth movements, armed by the Counsellor for Home Affairs of the Generalitat. The latter, Dencàs, wanted to keep the FAI out, and this body maintained the CNT in a state of ironic neutrality. The Barcelona working class, held thus to one side, was not given arms. When on 6 October Companys proclaimed, without much conviction, "the Catalan State within the Federal Republic", General Batet, the garrison commander, only needed 500 men and a few shells to obtain the surrender of the insurgents, cut off brusquely in their own headquarters (a traditional piece of tactics). In the countryside there were a few brutal incidents, but no general uprising. In Madrid, this defeat of the Catalans strengthened Lerroux. The Falange applauded him and Gil Robles rallied to the Republic!

In Asturias the movement started from below and was on the contrary marked by a revolutionary spirit of unity amongst the workers, this time with arms. Anarchists from Gijón, socialist miners and the communists (whose influence was increasing) forgot their quarrels in an "Alianza obrera" and rose against the Government on 5 October.

The centre of the revolt was located in the Mieres mines. The police barracks were stormed, then the arms factories at Trubia and Vega del Rey. Oviedo was taken by 8000 miners. Troops were thrown in, the Air Force began bombing. For nine days the town and surrounding district lived under a strict revolutionary régime, controlling both military and economic matters. But the area was soon surrounded. The army and the Civil Guard came down the passes, the Moroccan regiments of General López Ochoa disembarked on the coast. The revolutionaries had to disperse in the villages and mountains. Local leaders, insurgents and women covered their retreat with a desperate heroism. The whole episode had lasted fifteen days.

For a year the official press kept up daily the story of revolutionary "atrocities" while under cover frightening accounts of the repression circulated. Spain had had its "Commune", a terrible spectre for some, and for others an inspiring symbol of heroism and suffering amongst the workers.

(c) *October 1934 to February 1936*

Why, in February 1936, did the electoral pendulum swing back to the extreme Left? Certain major incidents occurring in the course of 1935 may serve to explain this. *First,* deflation, in the midst of complete economic decline. *Second,* the social reaction. The exceptional state of affairs after October provoked a brusque social response—dismissal of workers and salary cuts. In the countryside, particularly in Catalonia, the expulsion of tenants was hardly distinguishable from reprisals; agrarian reform was halted. Jiménez Fernández, a Christian socialist minister who had at least wanted to assist the Extremadura *yunteros* (landless labourers possessing a team of ploughing mules) to have access to land ownership was told by a deputy that if the minister's *encyclicals* took away his land, he would turn heretic. And most striking of all was the compensation (about 230 million) voted to the expropriated gentry of 1932. The

Left Wing declared the measure illegal and the peasants, forgetting their disappointment at the first *bienio*, rallied *en masse* to the "Popular Front". *Third*, the policy of the President of the Republic. Seven cabinets in a year and a half—what a paradox under an ultra-parliamentary constitution, even though the opposition was almost always illegal! This was the achievement of Alcalá Zamora, who disliked Lerroux and feared Right-wing excesses. In December 1935 he formed a centre cabinet to his taste (with Portela Valladares) so that he could later dissolve parliament and preside over new elections. The electoral campaign gave back liberty to the press, and this brought into play or accentuated other psychological forces. *Fourth*, the profound effect of the October repression. The Right wanted harsh measures, and Lerroux a few heads. Alcalá Zamora had saved the leaders, but allowed subordinates to be executed. As the press was now free, the tragedies experienced by the lower classes went into print. The campaigns against the insurgents boomeranged and October was sanctified—the bogy from then on was the Civil Guard and the Moorish troops. *Fifth*, scandals connected with Lerroux. Lerroux's entourage had a bad reputation and two scandals confirmed it—bribery over a case of gaming rights and excessive compensation in a colonial affair. More serious was the fact that certain important posts (in the Catalan Generalitat amongst others) had been conferred on individuals already discredited. During this period, the Spanish word for black market was coined (*estraperlo*). *Sixth*, the Gil Robles enigma. Gil Robles had alienated the monarchists by his rallies, and the fascists by his parliamentary beliefs. He was also distrusted by the republicans. Why had he demanded the Ministry of Defence? What was he plotting with Franco, his chief of staff? Why had the youth sections of his party been given, here and there, the duties of armed police? Why was his electoral campaign conducted under his name alone, to cries of "Jefe, jefe", with portraits four storeys high? There were many clear reasons for the formation of an anti-fascist *bloc*.

One can gather from this combination of circumstances why Azaña became popular again and why the "Popular Front" succeeded (it had been created between June and August 1935 after negotiations between trade-unions and Left-wing parties on a fourteen-point programme). On 16 February 1936 the elections produced, for the third time in six years, a brutal surprise.

3. FEBRUARY TO JULY 1936;
FROM THE ELECTIONS TO THE PRONUNCIAMIENTO

In point of fact, the Left was not considered to have much chance of success, as their militant leaders were in prison, local councils suspended and the campaign period limited. The Centre had most support: the Right had mobilised spectacularly "anti-revolutionary" opinions, forecast a gain of 300 seats and refused to modify the electoral law favourable to local majorities. The first round clearly indicated that the Popular Front (even if it obtained 50 per cent of the total vote) would get these majorities, and this crushing reversal was confirmed by partial elections. The symbolic allegiances of Gil Robles–Calvo Sotelo in Madrid and Lerroux–Cambó in Catalonia were defeated. Such was the confusion that authority was handed to Azaña in twenty-four hours. Provincial governors withdrew without waiting for their successors. The failure of the slogan "against the revolution" gave in fact a revolutionary slant to the elections, to the Cortes and to a programme in appearance more moderate than in 1931.

This unexpected shock provoked sporadic outbursts. In the villages the rumour ran "the priests have lost". Their allies must be disarmed and their petty persecutions avenged. Numerous assaults on churches, convents and Acción Popular headquarters followed. Agitation also started up once more in the countryside. The expelled tenant farmers returned to their lands and agrarian reform began again spontaneously. In three months, two provinces (Toledo, Badajoz) shared out 250,000 hectares—more than in the whole of Spain since 1900. Whole villages of 3000 inhabitants entered into open conflict with the Civil Guard. In the towns, this agitation had other aims—the freeing of detainees (there were 30,000 of them: the leaders were got out quickly but the women in the suburbs thought the process too slow) and "reparations" for previous reprisals.

The government in consequence was the object of severe criticism. Gil Robles and Calvo Sotelo painted a black picture of events (curiously magnified in the French electoral campaigns). The extreme Left Wing countered with an emotional but understandable reply: "Tell the October murderers to shut up". In fact, the authorities had only one idea in mind—to avoid another Casas Viejas, for the slightest sign of harshness would have unleashed a tragedy. Azaña had no wish to be cut off again from the people; but he did not lead, he followed. No positive encouragement was given to popular unrest and this was interpreted simply as a sign of impotence. Fascist organisations adopted the *pistolero* formula: the socialist vice-president of the Cortes was attacked and the magistrate who sentenced the attackers assassinated. One can see here, both in Parliament and in the streets, the old habits of the nineteenth century asserting themselves. A storm gathered round the head of the President of the Republic who ended up by antagonising everybody. When he was replaced by Azaña, the Left lost its only possible prime minister. A primeval atmosphere hovered over Madrid, recalling 1835; a rumour of poisoned sweets unleashed a furious outburst against the convents. It goes without saying that the generals were plotting—they had never ceased to do so since 1931. But when the communists called for the arrest of the most suspect amongst them (Goded and Franco), the government preferred to send them in disgrace to the Balearics and the Canaries—the classic excuse for every pronunci-amiento! The President of Council, Casares Quiroga, nevertheless declared himself "an enemy of fascism", and there was little doubt he knew a plot was being hatched. But he pretended it was only "café gossip". At that moment on 12 July Calvo Sotelo, the opposition leader, was assassinated by police officers to avenge (they said) the death of one of their republican comrades. This meant the government became a responsible party which could not dare to forbid opposing manifestations at the funerals of both victims. On 18 July the military rising took place.

III. THE CIVIL WAR (1936-39)

1. FROM THE PRONUNCIAMIENTO TO THE CIVIL WAR

A "pronunciamiento"? Never! "A national uprising" was the answer of the Franco régime to any query about the affair. But what a perfect example of the pronunciamiento took place on 18 July 1936!

For months army officers had been conspiring. Their chief was Sanjurjo, the exile responsible for the last plot, and he was linked to the politician, Calvo Sotelo. They had contacts in the garrisons, in the political parties, abroad (Germany, Italy, even England). They first planned for May, then late July, and finally decided to take advantage of the moral shock of Calvo Sotelo's murder. On 17 July the army in Morocco, deeply committed, gave the signal. On 18 July the generals in disgrace, Goded in the Balearics, Franco in the Canaries, took preliminary local steps and then proceeded to the centres of action, one to Barcelona, the other to Morocco. On the same day all the garrisons "pronounced", came out on to the streets and proclaimed "a state of war". In case of minor resistance, local authorities were to be countered with force, in the case of major resistance, opinion was divided amongst the military leaders. Some of these had only been persuaded by threats and success looked very chancy. In Seville, Queipo de Llano won over the garrison in a tragicomic fashion and then crushed the suburban areas; in Malaga, the Civil Governor carried the day; in Aragon police support meant certain victory for the "Movement"; in Barcelona the Civil Guard remained loyal. A traditionally defensive attitude was adopted in extreme situations—a show of loyalty to gain time and arms, then stubborn resistance to the besiegers. This was the case in Madrid at the Montaña barracks, in Toledo at the Alcázar, and with Colonel Aranda in Oviedo.

All this recalls the nineteenth century. But however technically successful the pronunciamiento may have been, it was its political failure at the nerve centres of the nation that transformed the situation into one of revolution and civil war. The *coup d'état* did in fact succeed, in the sense that it deprived the Republic of almost all its officers. No nineteenth-century government had been able to resist in such circumstances. But the *coup* failed in the sense that the army could only re-establish authority over a limited area. Elsewhere it was disarmed by the people and the government refused to recognise defeat, even in spite of the destruction of its military strength. This is where the great change occurred. Just as parliamentary methods without the masses failed to produce a government in 1932, so a pronunciamiento directed against the masses could not hope to get the upper hand.

For the first time the army did not mean simply the officers. In Madrid, Valencia and Barcelona the other ranks went over to the people when they got the chance. In four-fifths of the Navy's ships the sailors and petty officers executed and then replaced their rebellious commanders. The people ceased to be a shapeless mass; political parties, trade unions, youth groups formed cadres for popular militias as soon as the authorities agreed to accept their support. From that point on there existed a counterweight to the professional military leaders. Moreover, the regional *blocs* declared against the pronunciamiento, a direct result of Basque and Catalan nationalism. Finally the government found support (moral support at least) amongst the middle classes, more numerous now than in the nineteenth century, because it stood for legality against "España negra", the clergy and the generals, those traditional bogies of liberalism.

"España negra" was thus no longer the masses, but it had not disappeared by any means. General Mola rallied the carlists; the monasteries gave refuge to the insurgents and preached a "crusade"; the parties on the Right were ready to take over once again their position in the *bienio negro*; their youth groups, disillusioned with Gil Robles, went over to the fascists, but this time it was no longer an incidental scuffle between minorities. It was the beginning of civil war.

2. MILITARY OPERATIONS

Already by 20–21 July there emerged a military and geographical division favourable at the time to the government. Leaving aside

Morocco and the off-shore islands, the insurgents could only count on the mountain areas of Aragon, Navarre, Galicia, the meseta of Old Castile projecting as far as Cáceres, and the Andalusian coast from Algeciras to Huelva. Which of these separate stretches of territory would join up first? This was the aim of the initial military operations.

(a) The struggle for a united front

The insurgent area in Navarre and Castile was able to carry on a carlist-type campaign, but the outcome depended on the Moroccan shock troops. The Navy, antagonistic to the "movement", blocked the Straits. Here Franco, now in charge of the southern zone because of the accidental death of Sanjurjo, found support abroad. He was able to buy transport planes while Tangiers haggled over supplies to the government fleet—and this was scattered by Italian bombers at the appropriate moment. A few air transports, a landing at Algeciras and the major problems in the south were solved for Franco. On 14 August Yagüe's Moroccan column reached Badajoz, where the struggle ended in a massacre. The north–south link was established. At the same time Mola attacked Irún whose fall on 15 September isolated the Basque–Asturian front. Lacking their own shock troops, the government lost their first opportunity to keep the enemy disunited.

(b) The battle for Madrid

Victory could be said to lie with the possession of Madrid. Yagüe began the siege as soon as he had delivered Toledo (27 September). By late October, the capital was encircled on three sides and on 6 November it was abandoned by the government. On 7 November the Moors were at the bridges of the Manzanares, and two days later the general assault began. Amazingly it failed. From all sides reinforcements poured in. The International Brigades brought to the defence of the city the experience of the 1914 war, and the front was stabilised. Two other attempts failed—the Jarama attack (combined with a successful Italian offensive on Malaga) then a motorised thrust towards Guadalajara broken in counter-attack. From then on Madrid was free from assault.

(c) *Reduction of the isolated fronts*

The offensive against the Basque–Asturian zone began on 31 March 1937. This was distinguished by new ordeals—the heavy bombing of Durango and Guernica, and the failure of the fortifications around Bilbao, which fell on 19 June. The republicans responded with diversionary moves against Brunete (near Madrid, 5–24 July), and Belchite (Aragon, 3 September). In August the Italians took Santander and Asturias fell in October. The government was left with a third of national territory, but it held half the population. Although there was still hope, its economic difficulties were increasing.

(d) *The struggle in Aragon*

A major republican effort was launched in late 1937 and the taking of Teruel delayed until March 1938 a strong Francoist offensive to isolate Catalonia and cut Madrid off from the sea. Nevertheless, in April the first of these objectives was achieved—Catalonia was separated from Valencia at the Ebro estuary. In May and June the advance on Valencia passed Castellón, but it was held sharply when the government took the offensive on the Ebro on 24 July. The summer was spent in a deadlock of artillery barrages which recalled, for the first time, the First World War and in which the republican army of Catalonia wasted away (with, it was said, 80,000 casualties). Through November it was pushed yard by yard to the other side of the river, and in December came the final blow.

(e) *The fall of Catalonia and the end of the war*

The attack, with air-support, opened two breaches, exploited by motorised columns and rapid thrusts. This was a new type of warfare. The republican army, caught unawares and with little equipment, had to retire or be cut off. Barcelona fell on 26 January 1939 and in February the campaign drew to a close. Four hundred thousand refugees poured into France while the Negrín government retired to Valencia. Only the communists supported him in carrying on the war. An opposition Junta was formed in Madrid to negotiate a surrender, but it took several days of struggle before communist opposition was overcome. Franco was then able to order the occupation of Madrid on 28 March. The war had ended.

3. THE NATURE OF THE WAR

The transformation of a series of riots, small military engagements and guerrilla activity into the most modern warfare arose from military, social, national and international circumstances. The insurgent camp, with insufficient shock troops, had to mobilise and commission the youth of the leisured classes. Nevertheless, without equipment, naval or industrial backing, the modernisation of the army would have been impossible without foreign aid. The republicans had the support of the enthusiastic masses, the navy and the industrial regions. In a traditional Spanish war they would have had the upper hand, but only on condition that they had the time to reorganise an army. The officers, even the loyal ones, were suspect and the educated youngsters hardly reliable. Everything depended on the enthusiasm of the militant element, whose belief in the anarchist myth of "indiscipline" ("militia yes, soldiers no") had first to be exploded. This delayed for a long time mobilisation and unity of command. At the beginning the armed forces were a curious revolutionary breed, but once there was a real front, something else was needed. It was the communists who did most of the organisation work, training model regiments, officer training corps and backing those astonishing peoples' generals like Lister which Spain produced yet once again. The results were only seen tardily in 1938 under Negrín, when the fighting troops were already exhausted, the rearguard ill-fed and when an isolated Catalonia was incapable of furnishing modern equipment against a foreign enemy who was changing the nature of the war.

Foreign intervention had been responsible for the transformation. Mussolini's Italy effected a theatrical entry when its aeroplanes held the straits for Franco and Majorca fell under their control. The "Black Arrows" were present at Malaga, Guadalajara, in the north, Tortosa, and in the final campaign. Seventy thousand "volunteers" were paid half by Franco, half by Mussolini. Hitler's support, more discreet, was more selfish—it remained at the technical level, under German control. Technicians dealing with communications, radio, the DCA, the Air Force, came for periods of six months under secret orders. In 1940 pilots counted their exploits in Spain in their service record while the Catalan campaign provided the necessary technical experience for the later motorised campaigns in Poland and France.

On the other side, only Russian support was openly confessed: the despatch of technicians (few in number) and the supply of out-dated but plentiful and well-constructed materiel was hampered by distance and intermediary handling. In England, the Chamberlain attitude and big business interests, in France a veritable moral civil war gave rise on one hand to the inefficient legal arrangement of "non-intervention" and on the other to a struggle between propaganda sources, political media, camouflaged consignments and the various sympathies of civil servants. The republicans were able to recruit volunteers and acquire material (not without interruptions), but this could not match the massive Italian and German intervention.

In this game Spain in 1936 became, like Spain in 1808, the theatre of world-wide passion and despair. By reason of this fact, its history is difficult to write. We shall only try to relate each of the two Spains with the problems we have posed in this book and attempt to distinguish between the word and the spirit, between the public act and the underlying reality.

4. THE INTERNAL EVOLUTION OF THE TWO SPAINS (1936–39)

(a) *Political evolution*

The reconstruction of authority, the conciliation of new and old formulae—this was the political problem in both camps (subordinated of course to the necessities of war, local resources and foreign opinion).

In *the republican zone*, on 18 July, one authority confronted another in the traditional Spanish manner. The "cantonalism" of 1873 emerged once again in Aragon and Upper Catalonia. The Catalan government, faced with workers in arms, underwrote a non-marxist trade-union revolution based on local initiative. In Madrid, and then Valencia, where the masses were either communist or socialist, Giral wanted to preserve legality while later Largo Caballero attempted a revolutionary coalition. After some tentative moves, the search for an expression of authority came to rest on a new man, the socialist professor Negrín, supported by communist groups who were gaining ground through their discipline, their activities at the front, and the prestige of Russian aid. There were several stages in this evolution—May 1937, street-fighting in Barcelona against an anarchist movement; September, the installation of Negrín in Barcelona and the trial of the POUM (a breakaway communist group). Discipline won through when resources were exhausted and after the fall of Catalonia Negrín was removed by a coalition of moderates, anarchists and military leaders. The anti-fascists certainly suffered from their lack of unity.

The "*Movement*" was more amenable to political direction. Not that it was any less divided, but the conservative mass accepted the authority of the clergy and the army, and top-level struggles were concealed from them. General Franco (promoted to leadership through the disappearance of Sanjurjo) Calvo Sotelo, José Antonio and then Mola were lucky enough to find themselves at the focal point of many tendencies and clever enough to stay there. Franco left propaganda and local issues to the young fascists, reassured the Church, the "traditionalists" and the landowners, while preparing above all to get control of the army. But it was a long time before he gave precise outlines to the régime.

In October 1936 a classic "Junta de Defensa" was replaced by "Generalissimo" Franco and his "Technical Junta". Discussions over the creation of a "single party" lasted until April 1937. It had a complex title: "Falange Española Tradicionalista y de las Juntas de Ofensiva Nacional Sindicalistas" (FET y JONS). In August 1937 Franco was proclaimed *caudillo* and also Head of State. In January 1938 the Junta became a cabinet. The basic principles of the régime, however, were a post-war product. The crises (like the elimination of the carlists and intransigent falangists) were kept hidden for a long time, and have only come to light in recent times.

Franco's main strength lay in the fact that both inside and out, the counter-revolutionary coalition stayed firm. Despite a few doctrinal scruples, the Church made shift with the fascist programme, and foreign capital provided financial backing for Franco. Assured of moral and economic guarantees, the régime screened its brutality at home and prepared for a double game abroad.

(b) *"Terrorist" repression*

It would be absurd to underestimate the acts of violence which still dominate the memory of the average Spaniard today. These acts, terrifying because of the lack of premeditation on the part of the "Reds", and equally terrifying when carried out regularly and methodically by the "Whites", have frequently provoked judgements which may be in need of revision.

One must bear in mind that in certain aspects these events reflect a Spanish temperament. There were priests who blessed the worst of fusillades, mobs who hurled monks and nuns into their graves. It was the clash of a faith and an anti-faith which drew their ideas on death and sacrilege from the same sources: ideas which had been kept alive in the hot-house of the Counter Reformation from the fifteenth century fought against the craving for liberation—Goya's *Caprichos*, Unamuno's *agonías*, Bunuel's films—a constant, anguished, spasmodic and fratricidal war with the past.

There are also certain figures which need to be examined: a million dead, 20,000 clerics killed, a massive "White Terror". This is plain illusion. Three anarchists have produced for me the following figures on the Francoist executions in Saragossa: five shot, 14,000, or at least 30,000 casualties. Demographic calculations lead one to believe that the population loss due to the Civil War is in the region of 560,000, including both war and bombing casualties. Of course, it must not be thought that an adjustment of the figures lessens the emotional impact. It is this impact which weighed heavily after the war.

The psychological effect of an uncontrolled, spectacular "Red Terror", striking down well-known figures, cannot be set aside. The régime exploits it daily in the press, by acts of remembrance and a well-worn phraseology. However, public opinion is equally aware of the terror unleashed by the "Movement" either on falangist or military instigation. From the earliest days this terror struck even those who held divergent opinions no less savagely than in popular acts of repression; and it lasted far longer than the revolutionary outburst. It followed in the wake of the advancing armies and persisted into the post-war years. It restrained many opponents of violence from rallying to Franco, and the spectacle of prisons, prison camps and moral coercion is still witness to its existence.

Despite all this, the root cause lies elsewhere, in a national and social crisis which was so universally evident in 1936 that both sides called for a patriotic defence of the mother country and a revolutionary spirit. Let us see what diversity of intention lay behind these common expressions.

(c) *The problem of nationality*

The psychological reaction of Basques and Catalans was deeply "national" in the sense that group feeling drew together fervent Catholics and militant anticlericals. In both areas, major bourgeois figures who forgot their "national past" to engage in class warfare, were treated as traitors, an attitude which bound regional sentiment even closer to the defence of democracy. These emotions went back to the federal tradition, not in itself alien to the anarchist outlook. And communism, for its part, agreed to support any truly popular regional movement as long as it did not impede, but reinforced the struggle.

On the other hand, German and Italian intervention was detested in the republican zone as a violation of liberty and the native soil. Anarchist speakers were heard to invoke 1808 and the Reconquest. There was talk of a National Front. Ever since Giner's time the intellectuals had sought to fuse tradition and innovation. From Antonio Machado to Alberti, Altolaguirre and Hernández, the poets offered to the people at war "ballads", satires and songs with all the more emotion since the greatest amongst them, Federico García Lorca, one of the most amazing poets of all time, had been executed in Granada, the first victim of the military campaign. The landscape, the art, the history of Spain were extolled by educational and propaganda departments. The far-sighted rested their hopes on a new patriotism, linked to popular aspirations and without hostility to regional ideals, to resolve the national crisis.

Nationalism in the other camp was quite different. It was above all unitarian and aggressive in intention. The Falange and the JONS confessed their debt to the fascist mystique of unity. In the Spanish context this meant no local nationalisms. "All separatism is a crime which we shall never pardon", said the Falange, hoping thus to canalise the one deep-seated fear of the Spanish body politic, that of dissolution. However, in order to proscribe the Catalans and the Basques it was necessary to remove from the word "nation" the romantic, Mistralian sense of spontaneous community feeling. Since Spain's grandeur belonged to history, then Spain had a "historical unity" deemed inseparable from a "permanent, transcendent, supreme and destined unity of purpose" (for, of course, "historical" could mean "variable"). Its guarantee would be pride of caste, equivalent to the Nazi pride of race. The Spanish *hidalgo*, the *caballero cristiano* was esteemed for his "style of life", dictated by a "poetic imperative". This was also the goal of certain literary currents like the rehabilitation of Don Quixote and a mystical, warlike *casticismo*.

This "nationalism" was in consequence hardly accessible to the masses. The average Franco partisan was moved by older habits of mind—the peasant tradition, military patriotism (overjoyed by the return of the yellow and red flag and the Royal March) the confusion of faith and fatherland (encouraged by the clergy), as well as the facile success of conformist intellectuals who drew on the arsenals of erudition assembled by the American historian Pereyra or Menéndez y Pelayo. So propaganda changed abruptly from the restive nationalism of José Antonio who wanted to see the "physical wreck" of Spain rise upwards "along the road of self-criticism", into a self-satisfied vanity whose favourite argument was the historical cliché.

On the other hand, the Falange had launched a stirring "imperial" programme, claiming Gibraltar, Tangiers, French Morocco and the leadership of the "Spanish axis" as against Anglo-Saxon Panamericanism. This did make an impact in the period of German successes. But when events obliged Spanish diplomacy and propaganda first to dissemble and then to rally hurriedly to the previously despised "democracies", this fresh failure deprived the nationalist elements in the régime of the dynamic power on which they had relied. Campaigns against other Spaniards (exiles, separatists), against France, "the enemy of tradition", against distant Russia, were carried out in the vain hope of recovering the impetus.

(d) *The problem of social change*

Would deep social changes emerge from this bloody conflict? In the republican zone the upheaval came rapidly—not that there weren't any conservatives amongst the republicans. But just as the failure of the 1932 pronunciamiento had led to the only radical agrarian measure of the Republic, so it was assumed that the reaction to the rising of 18 July would end in social revolution.

While workers' committees assumed control of business firms and municipalities, the trade unions took over major public services. The peasants occupied land or left off paying rent. The FAI and CNT launched isolated "libertarian" experiments in Aragon and Catalonia which often coincided with the principles of traditional "agrarian collectivism". In October 1936 the Generalitat sanctioned a wide measure of industrial collectivisation, obligatory in the case of units with more than a hundred employees, optional in average firms (from fifty to a hundred), and automatically applicable to any firm on account of bankruptcy or political activity by the management. An Economic Board was to supervise national planning.

In the rest of republican Spain important measures were taken in the agrarian sector. A decree of October 1936 systematised those already widely applied by the peasants—subdivision of large estates and confiscation on account of abandonment or political activity. The choice between collectivisation or individual working was left to local communities. In May 1938 the following figures were published: 2,432,202 hectares confiscated because of abandonment or political reasons, 2,008,000 for the benefit of the nation and 1,252,000 provisionally taken over subject to revision. A programme of financial support, technical aid, planned farming and mechanisation was forecast by the Institute for Agrarian Reform. But it had no time to implement it. In Andalusia and Extremadura agriculture lacked both means and experience, and production was maintained only in areas run by co-operatives, smallholders or tenant farmers. The main problem was the organisation of controls imposed by a war economy.

In addition the attitudes of political parties and trade-unions in face of these new situations varied considerably. The communists, who believed that victory was a condition of revolution and subordinated everything to the war effort, refused to attack smallholders and condemned indiscriminate collectivisation. The dissident communists and the anarchists, believing that total revolution was a condition of victory, saw betrayal in any restriction of their earlier plans. Recent studies have thrown light on some of those experiments, none of which have left any significant trace. However, all bore witness to the need for a profound change in the structure of Spanish society.

This need appeared sufficiently pressing in 1936 for the pronunciamiento (whose programme had been negative) to feel obliged to

adopt in the early stages of the war the "twenty-six points" of the
Falange, a Spanish version of the fascist ideology which had recently
disturbed the moderates with its theoretical condemnation of
established order—"We repudiate capitalism", "We cannot tolerate
the poverty of the masses while a few enjoy luxury", "Spain will be
nacional-sindicalista". These were terms which allowed them to
imitate the Nazis without copying them and to recall at the same
time the Spanish corporative practices, and even (a change from
1923) to flirt with anarcho-syndicalism, "the gunman in the mackin-
tosh", "more Spanish" than the disciplined and materialist Marxist,
who had now become public enemy number one.

Can one see here a precise economic doctrine? The formulae are
vague—"the correction of the faults of capitalism", refusal to accord
"the slightest consideration" to non-productive elements. On
certain points the ideology is contradictory; "a trade union of producers" suggests a society based on labour, but there was support
also for José Antonio's view that such a basis was materialist, anti-
Spanish and anti-Christian (work is travail and not fulfilment; life
should be guided by the militant religious spirit).

There were denunciations of the *señorito*, the upper class idler, but
he had responded to the appeal of the caste and enlisted. Condemned
as a *señorito* he was nevertheless praised as an *hidalgo*. What revolutionary pledge can one extract from his defensive war? By glorifying
"Old Spain" in its "refusal" of the sixteenth- and eighteenth-century
revolutions, "New Spain" was led to declare itself implicitly counter-
revolutionary, and no one doubted it could be otherwise. Despite
the vocabulary of the Falange, the masses who fell in behind Franco
were those who in February voted "against revolution" either
through tradition or self-preservation.

Franco himself, although he intended to turn the dynamism of
the Falange to his own ends, at first employed more moderate
phrases—"social justice", "the teachings of the Church", "bread for
all and a fire on every hearth". In 1938, when the Party achieved
unity, he finally promulgated the "Fuero del Trabajo" which calls
for some comment.

The word *fuero* here is a gesture to tradition and the historical consciousness, and not without some abuse of the term. The medieval *fuero* was a strict contract between authority and the community, both precisely defined—the new *fuero* is a declaration of rights without any sanction. Furthermore the "Fuero del Trabajo" represents a clear retreat from the Falange programme. Its social pledges were modest (holidays, insurance, basic wages), and if one can speak of a plan to create a "vertical syndicate" under the leadership of the Party, the agrarian issue went by the board. In contrast to Italian fascism, based on large-scale industry and more flexible in agrarian matters, Spanish fascism was intent on gaining control of industry (the Basque and Catalan managerial class remained suspect) without frightening agrarian interests.

The practical measures taken during the war can be seen under various lights. First came a reversal of the work of the Popular Front—wages held to February 1936 level, estates restored to their owners (those peasants who had been settled for some time and who were not suspect could remain as tenants), compensation for those whose property had been affected for political reasons. Certain *de facto* acts preceded legislation, such as falangist trade-union control of business firms. On the other hand legislative measures were passed and not applied, like social insurance, confiscation of uncultivated estates. To this must be added the imposition of a war economy which was to have an impact in later years—the controlled distribution of industrial material, a national wheat plan administered by a single agrarian syndicate which laid down areas to be sown and took over the complete harvest. The most obvious social measures were also circumstantial—reconstruction work and compensation for war victims, an "Auxilio Social" which attempted to cover up the most visible poverty by a spectacular charity campaign. The introduction of charity as a social remedy responded, it is true, to a traditional practice which forms the basis of the social outlook of upper class Spaniards. If the Church had some reserves it was because the mobilisation of good works by the women of the nation reminded one more of Hitler than of tradition.

In short, far from unleashing a "revolution" as defined in falangist terms, the war did not bring about any profound change of social

structure in the nationalist zone. On the contrary, the ruling classes
—the clergy, the army, the *jeunesse dorée*, linked either with the
Party, the military cadres or Auxilio Social—established themselves
decisively without any new economic formulae coming into play.
Would it be the same after the war?

IV. THE REGIME OF GENERAL FRANCO (1939-75)

In the two score years or so of its existence, various phases can be
discerned.

1. *1939–42*. Before May 1940 Franco was concerned to regroup
the so-called "Western Powers" against the USSR. When the
German army triumphed in Europe he moved from neutrality to
"non-belligerence" (13 June), occupied Tangiers, lent his support
to the Germanophile Serrano Suñer, had a meeting with both
Hitler and Mussolini. In exchange for a dramatic show of sympathy
he expected material aid and colonial expansion. But Ribbentrop
and Hitler showed little inclination to open a second front in
hazardous terrain. A meeting between Spain and Portugal (February
1942) assured both the Allies and the Axis of Iberian neutrality, and
within Spain it was a difficult period of isolation and deprivation.
The Falange imposed an economic policy and legislation derived
from Nazi models.

2. *1942–44*. The landings in North Africa forced General Jordana,
Serrano Suñer's successor, to yield to Allied pressure. His offers of
reconciliation with the West were not well received, but Spain did
receive supplies from abroad for her manufacturing industries. At
the same time the vocabulary of totalitarianism was damped down.

3. *1944–48*. After the Allied victory Spanish Foreign policy under
Lequerica and subsequently Martín Artajo evaded advice about
democratisation while at the same time offering support for
American initiatives. However, the state of international opinion

forced UNO to denounce Franco and France was obliged to close
the common frontier. The Spanish government, in an atmosphere
of inflation and poverty, attempted and failed to whip up a national
reaction. The bad conscience of the régime was made evident by
the way the dictatorship was camouflaged as a regency while
Franco juggled for support from Falangists, Catholics and negotiated
with Don Juan.

4. *1948–55.* However, the cold war did permit Franco as one of
the survivors of fascism to parade himself as a fore-runner of an
anti-communist bloc. He acted towards the USA as he had done
towards Germany—in the role of creditor rather than debtor. The
USA in turn hoped to use Spain rather than be used by her. In 1953
military aid worth 141 million dollars was offered plus 85 million
"to strengthen the economic bases of military cooperation". The
concurrent signing of a Concordat with Rome meant that the
régime could boast of a successful foreign policy.

5. *1956–62.* The initial stages of economic revival and industrialisation were accompanied by inflation and consequently by marked
social disturbances, particularly in the universities. Nevertheless,
Spain entered UNO and other European organisations. A
"Stabilisation Plan" in 1959–60 restrained currency losses, but also
brought about a recession. 1962 was again a year of strikes and
demonstrations, particularly in Asturias.

6. *1963–73.* This was a period of lively growth stimulated by a
series of "Plans". The régime celebrated two and a half decades of
existence with the slogan of *veinticinco años de paz,* while the new
"Organic Law" of 1966 maintained Franco as head of state and
the Cortes as a corporate body. It was submitted to a general
referendum during which the failure of a policy of abstention
promoted by the opposition, together with official measures taken
to smother anti-Franco activity, threw up a total of voters in support
which was greater than the number on the official voting registers.
Censorship, it is true, was legally disposed of, but this was matched
by an increase in the number of convictions for improper publica-

tions. In July 1970 Prince Juan Carlos was accorded an official post
as successor designate to Franco, a form of monarchical restoration
disapproved of by both the carlists and Don Juan. In December, the
Burgos terrorist trials which sought the death penalty for six young
members of ETA (a nationalist Basque organisation in open revolt
against the police) provoked a wave of protest. Franco exercised his
right of clemency which led to other demonstrations by partisans
of the hard line. From that point on the technocrats of the Opus
Dei seemed to have displaced the falangists in power. Nevertheless,
Admiral Carrero Blanco in his new role as prime minister remained
an intransigent authoritarian. On 20 December 1973 in the middle of
Madrid, his car was blown up, an act for which ETA claimed
responsibility. The death of the prime minister was not a matter of
universal regret, and despite an apparent atmosphere of tranquillity,
the crisis of the régime was evident.

7. *1974–75.* In these years the economic climate ceased to be
promising. The revolution in Portugal provoked both fear and hope.
The health of General Franco led to rumours about succession and
a flurry of intrigue enveloped official circles. The new prime minister Arias Navarro announced a series of political reforms
concerning political associations which in the end amounted to
nothing, but many supporters of the régime moved into the
opposition camp. Here and there political activity flared up and the
press voiced criticism. Repression inevitably hardened: a young
anarchist Puig Antich was executed in March 1974: the death
penalty and torture was meted out to members or supposed
accomplices of ETA and FRAP (*Frente Revolucionaria, Antifascista y
Patriótica*). Eleven were condemned and five executed in September
1975. The régime thus remained faithful to its origins.

Had it in any way resolved the main problems facing Spain?

The problem of the national framework is still without solution.
Separatism had always been the *bête noire* of the Falange. In the
years 1955–60 Madrid allowed certain manifestations of the various
regional cultures. The Catalan version of this policy had an extraordinary success. The Catalan language became again the flag of

combat, flown more vigorously than ever in Valencia, the Balearics and Roussillon. The pace-makers as always were the clergy and the intellectuals, and bourgeois elements rediscovered in 1975 the slogans of 1906. In the working-class quarters of Barcelona, Sabadell and Terrassa national and social grievances ran together once again. A "Catalan Assembly", officially proscribed and hotly debated amongst the radicals, demonstrated its power to mobilise a wide range of opinion which remained despite all moderate in tone. By contrast, in the Basque Provinces national aspirations, led by a youthful minority, took a harder line. ETA (*Euzkadi ta askatasuna*—the Basque Country and liberty), although torn by dispute over theory and tactics, drew attention to itself through the heroism of its fighters in the streets, in the torture chambers, in the law-courts and in their linking of national liberty and social revolution. They sowed fear in other opposition groups and successfully imposed their authority.

1. AGRICULTURE AND INDUSTRIALISATION

What of economic issues? Twenty years of stagnation followed by a dramatic expansion call for a balanced analysis. Let us consider *agriculture* first. Up to 1962 the "inequality of yield" in harvest figures had not altered. In 1958 wheat production in thousands of metric tons was 4800, in 1961 it was 3000. These were below the average figures for 1931–35. The available cereal consumption per head dropped 35 per cent and the production value per agricultural worker 18 per cent. In 1960, 47 per cent of the active population were still engaged in agriculture; it accounted for 33 per cent of the gross national product, but only for 13 per cent of total investment. Experiments in agricultural settlements (Badajoz, 35 villages) were localised. There were still men without land, land without men, and land crammed with men.

In 1962 modernisation took off. The mean production figure for wheat went from 4000 metric tons (1954–58) to 5000 (1965–69), the yield rose from 9·4 to 12·5 quintals per hectare. Maize, barley, pigs and poultry have developed rapidly. Fertilisers have been extensively and massively utilised. In 15 years the number of tractors has gone from 26,000 to 243,000. But can the *latifundia* system offer a satisfactory basis for expansion? The rural exodus has gone beyond a comfortable peak, investment is still insufficient (15 dollars per hectare as against 60 in Europe) and markets are uncertain. The decline of agriculture as part of the gross national product (from 33 to 15 per cent) or as part of the active labour force (42 to 26 per cent) is a significant trend, but a costly one over the past 10 years. This economic metamorphosis has not been able to solve the social problems of *minifundia* either, or of wages, rural unemployment and abandoned villages.

Industrialisation was also slow to come but rapid in take off. Up to 1951–53 the INI (National Industrial Institute) applied an autarchic falangist economic policy to the advantage of the centre of the Peninsula. 55,000 million pesetas were invested up to 1960, of which 42,000 went into basic industries (electricity, petroleum, iron and steel), without, however, righting the regional imbalance, nor expanding sufficiently the role of power and steel. Export of raw material continued.

From 1954 to 1962 autarchy yielded to open intervention by foreign capital; dirigisme gave way to liberal economics. The European boom and aid from the USA (1954–58: 341 million dollars of which 31 were for electricity, 30 for railways, 8 for irrigation) converged to create an inflationist situation and an adverse trading balance (1951–54: imports from the USA rose from 62 to 112 million dollars while exports to the USA fell from 65 to 46). Price rises were steep; from 1956 to 1957 the rise was 15·5 per cent. The stabilisation plan of 1959 was paid for in 1960–61 by putting the brakes on growth.

In 1961 the national consumption of power and steel did not reach a third of the mean for OEEC countries. In seven years the gross national product had only risen by 18 per cent. It is true that the industrial index figure went up rapidly because of expansion in certain sectors (cars, aluminium), but this should not lead to any convictions about overall growth which only became manifest in 1962.

From 1964 to 1969 the gross national product climbed by 35

per cent and income per head by 28 per cent (an irregular movement—1964–65 : 6·7 per cent; 1966–67 : 3 per cent). The consumption of power doubled in 10 years (also a jerky process from 0·06 to 10·9 per cent according to the years). In 1969 Spain produced 6 million tons of steel and consumed 8 million. So that in 1969 the ultimate results were modest—an income of 720 dollars per head, 1600 kilowatt hours per head of electricity or an equivalent of 1·38 tons of coal. In 1972 the corresponding figures were 1239 dollars, 2030 kilowatt hours and 1·79 tons of coal.

Towns have changed. In Burgos, Valladolid, Pamplona, Saragossa the outskirts have mushroomed. Madrid has become an industrial city, grey and polluted. Barcelona and Bilbao maintain their position in the pattern of national industry and have acquired vast suburban accretions. This explosive expansion has been managed by banks, both commercial and deposit. Foreign capital plays an increasingly significant role but is tied in closely with the interests of the ruling clique.

There are disturbing aspects: (a) the exodus of labour, often highly trained, (b) the place of the hotel and tourist trade in an uncertain climate of investment, (c) the growth of imports, (d) inflationary pressures.

2. THE SOCIAL SITUATION

Social problems still remain acute. For 15 years (1940–55) the working class was held down with no relief, enormous capital has accumulated and this the banks will certainly invest. Then the economic take-off will expose social disparities. In the countryside, the *minifundia* creates a poverty-stricken existence; the *latifundia* pays better, but the labourer, caught between emigration or unemployment, cannot quit the proletariat. On the other hand, there have emerged rich peasant sectors while in industry retarded areas like the Asturian mines are threatened with labour cuts and export crises hang over low salaried industries like clothing and footwear. New sectors have experienced concentration, salary differentiation, bonus rewards, overtime and double employment in the vain pursuit of rising prices. Labour conflicts have been frequent and prolonged despite the illegality of strikes. The official "vertical" trade-unions, under severe pressure, have only served to camouflage serious differences of opinion at the same time as the illegal "workers' committees" (*comisiones obreras*) have promoted debate and argument. Clandestine groups have disputed the initiative and often the clergy has offered refuge for their meetings. In consequence repression has been bloody, in Granada, El Ferrol, Madrid and Barcelona.

3. POLITICAL OPPOSITION

What part has the political opposition played in all this?

From 1940 to 1950–53 it never disappeared. There have always been local guerrilla movements, clandestine trade-unions, disillusioned falangists, unrepentant liberals, impatient monarchists. But they have made little impact. The old nuclei of opposition have died in prison or in exile. The middle classes, apprehensive of the future, have settled for purely verbal skirmishes. The image of a Spain "unproductive by nature", condemned to a series of arbitrary régimes relieved only by negligence or anarchy, has been bodied forth by the intellectuals in sceptical and pessimistic terms.

Even after 1944, liberalisation was a mere game of words. The Cortes were neither a parliament nor an assembly of estates. Neither the *Fuero de los Españoles* nor the *Fuero del Trabajo* offered individual guarantees. Fascist and Nazi influence left profound traces on the press, the police and youth organisations. When the economic revival stimulated a mass opposition, repressive action was adjusted according to the quality of the opponents.

We have mentioned the open belligerence of the working-class and the consequent retaliation in the street and in the factory. An intellectual opposition has been tolerated as the situation permitted, but it has suffered censorship, prison sentences or been exposed to the provocations of semi-official activists (wrecking of libraries, exhibitions). A poetry of social concern (Celaya, Blas de Otero), sombre and pessimistic novels, violently critical films (Bardem, Berlanga, Bunuel, Ferreri) summoned up once again the vision of *España negra;* the major universities lived in an atmosphere of permanent siege while the sons of well-known figures were active in opposition. And from the seventies there has been no lack of defections even in the higher échelons of the system—openly dissident theoreticians like Calvo Serer, or propagandists like Fraga Iribarne in search of an acceptable opposition.

In face of this erosion, the heirs of older parties and a profusion of new ones struggled for position, even though the paralysing memory of the past was still powerful. Was civil war avoidable, was it fatal? This was the persistent question of the moderates. Who was right (or rather who was wrong) asked the vanquished —the anarchists, the communists, the socialists, the bourgeois parties? The smaller groups had plenty of opportunity to blame the others, since their methods had not had to be put to the test. And the younger elements offered dogmatic solutions to situations they had not lived through. Much vitality but no less confusion.

In 1962 the appearance of Gil Robles at an international gathering in Munich suggested the possible emergence of a centre grouping with European links. The régime reacted flexibly to the move and with little risk to itself. On the other hand, the execution of the communist leader Julián Grimau demonstrated clear official intransigeance *vis-à-vis* wartime communism. In certain quarters this was reckoned to be a final settlement of accounts.

From that time on, divisions between communists, reborn anarchists, trotskyites and a revolutionary Basque party created an extreme left too fragmented to be decisive and too active to be ignored. The end of the expansionist mirage, the successful assassination of Carrero Blanco, the recent Portuguese revolution, all led to strange détentes and sudden harsh reactions. The garroting of Puig Antich and eleven death penalties in September 1975 provoked reprisals on the police force by ETA and the marxist-leninist cell of FRAP. This repressive apparatus has remained the soul of the régime.

The most significant change of attitude since 1936 has been that of the clergy. Priests have engaged in political activity and the authorities have not hesitated to strike back. In brief, the real choice for any opposition lies between two possibilities: a simple return to democratic practices (alas, the words "free world" and "the West" have been of great service to Franco), or a revolution in the social patterns of production. The Spanish communist party has chosen the former, the "Italian approach", and criticised the actions of the Portuguese Communist party; it has sought its allies within a *Junta Democrática* and associated with figures like Calvo Serer. This has brought reproaches from the "anti-revisionists"—but when the carlists turn socialist, who can escape contradiction? In the labyrinth of the class war, the régime has been able to see its enemies more clearly than its adversaries.

Is the conservative coalition a solid one?

The aristocracy, the great landowners, now closely tied to banking and industry, have little of the spirit of former days. The restoration of monarchy only matters in as much as it can guarantee law and order, under a liberal or authoritarian banner as the occasion demands.

The army and the forces of repression are still a constituent part of the system, forged as they were in and for civil war and continuously favoured by the Caudillo. In a country with few foreign problems, the weight of the army is paradoxical—it recalls the situation of the non-productive classes in the classic period of decline in the seventeenth century. The junior officer-classes and the police forces have been a refuge from poverty. Is this ill-paid mass sufficiently cohesive? We do not know. The officers have not forgotten the risks they ran in 1931, and it is unlikely they will follow the Portuguese example, itself a consequence of decolonisation. But sporadic manifestations have occurred, and may occur again.

Business circles would like to jettison the last fetters of dirigsme inherited from the forties. But for a truly liberal "boom", Spain is not Germany. A bourgeois régime will have less chance with a freely functioning parliamentary and electoral system. Industry and banking are not likely to risk their necks. Franco was clever enough in 1969 to sacrifice for the moment the Falange to the technocrats linked openly or covertly with the Opus Dei. The losers attempted to exploit in their favour the "Matesa" affair (fictitious exports attracting millions in state aid), but capitalist solidarity at home and abroad is not vulnerable to incidents like this. As soon as political threats take a revolutionary turn, a repressive mentality summons up its own defences. It is true that economic success has been both cause and effect of the social upsurge of intelligent technocrats who have flirted, are flirting and will flirt with "democratic" opposition groups who can be neutralised with either threats or favours.

The Church is now far removed from the time when it enjoyed success as the principal beneficiary of the "Crusade"—tax exemptions, church marriage as the only valid ceremony, the catechism imposed in schools, a dominant role in education, universities and research. The identification of the régime with a narrow catholicism has given way to three new trends: (a) The Opus Dei, a new type of religious order, is ambitious to mould lay society and has already played a decisive role as intermediary between official bodies, state capitalism, the technocrats of economic planning and the personnel of banking and industry. (b) On the other hand, youthful clergy from the suburban estates, even country priests, reacting against yesterday's conformity and today's ambition, have rediscovered a traditional climate of anticapitalism. (c) Between such currents the prelacy manoeuvres and the masses hesitate. All in all, *la España negra* has been dispersed.

However, none of the fundamental problems facing Spain, national, spiritual or social, has yet been resolved. The thought of a permanent conflict hidden under the garb of official Spain serves to maintain, in one sense, the established order of things. It never fails to rally, at home or abroad, the instinct of conservative blocs. In consequence the opposition parties feel that they must present themselves as united as possible, only excluding the ultras, and show themselves as capable of replacing peacefully an outworn political régime. The régime in turn reacts, and, as in the thirties, the young intensify their revolutionary impatience and political dogmatism.

The economic thrust with its irregularities, distortions and crises, cannot by itself settle all these difficulties. Spain in 1975 has to support 35 million inhabitants. Technology may get round old obstacles, but social difficulties need more than a team of politicians. Ten years ago one of the technocrats imprudently suggested that with a gross national product of a thousand dollars per head, Spain would become a democracy. That figure has now been left behind and the dream has not come true. Indeed the class struggle is sharper. As for the national framework, Spain must find a system of relations between the provinces other than that of an ill-received authoritarianism. She should also admit that her spiritual qualities, deeply original in themselves, are more complex and more inventive than those thrown up by a superficial nationalism or a shallow religious fervour.

The great crises of 1931, 1934, 1936, with their own heritage of confused and tragic issues from the past, have nevertheless highlighted a number of significant changes, later masked by a class dictatorship. The Spanish masses no longer accept willingly the rule of privileged minorities or narrow élites. It would be therefore unwise to imagine a future on the basis of patterns already a hundred years old—feuds, dynastic incidents, conspiracies by more or less clandestine groups. The press and diplomatic circles will always give space to these trivial clashes. Now the stakes are much higher. It is a question of the material and spiritual renewal of one of the most glorious historical creations in Europe. Great figures, like Falla, Lorca, Picasso, to name only the dead, have already expressed the exultation of this rebirth. Through them the Spanish contribution to the European sensibility of the twentieth century stands in the first rank, and through them one knows that the profound creative spirit of the Spaniards has nothing to fear from the future. One opportunity was hailed in 1936 in the glow of a popular movement: a fusion of tradition and innovation is still possible, as it is between the will of the nation (even if there is more than one) and the will to revolution. In December 1970, in September 1975, a young generation, armed the dual ideal of motherland and revolution, faced up to the antique apparatus of the military tribunal. Contrary to the title of the film by Semprún and Resnais, "la guerre n'est pas finie". For the first time since the prelude to the Second World War was played out on her territory, Spain has become one of the sensitive spots on the map of the world: there are few today who do not feel in some way linked with her future fate.

INDEX

133

138